OLIVIER
IN CELEBRATION

Drawing by Antony Sher
Key on page 209

OLIVIER
IN CELEBRATION

EDITED BY
GARRY O'CONNOR

Dodd, Mead & Company
NEW YORK

First published in the United States by Dodd, Mead & Company in 1987.

Published by Dodd, Mead & Company, Inc.
71 Fifth Avenue, New York, N.Y. 10003
Manufactured in the United States of America
First published in Great Britain by Hodder and Stoughton Limited, 1987.

First Edition

1 2 3 4 5 6 7 8 9 10

Library of Congress Cataloging-in-Publication Data

Olivier: in celebration / edited by Garry O'Connor.
     p.   cm.
   Includes index.
  1. Olivier, Laurence. 1907-   2. Actors—Great Britain-
-Biography.   3. Theatrical producers and directors—Great Britain-
-Biography. I. O'Connor, Garry. II. Olivier, Laurence. 1907-
PN2598.05504   1987
792′.028′0924—dc19
[B]   87-26337
ISBN 0-396-09212-8   CIP

CONTENTS

ILLUSTRATIONS

The Editor and the Publishers thank Adrian Woodhouse for generously lending his help in selecting the Angus McBean photographs.

The John Vickers photographs appear by permission of the John Vickers Archive, London.

INTRODUCTION

INTRODUCTION

GARRY O'CONNOR

"Hell take these Gascons! Why can't he get on that saffron horse of his and be off!"

"Not till I've killed you, you coward!" cried d'Artagnan, fighting back hard against his three assailants who were plastering him with blows. "Another of these swaggerers!" answered the stranger. "God, these Gascons are incorrigible!"

Like Charles de Batz-Castelmore, on whom Dumas based his swashbuckling character of d'Artagnan, Olivier has the heart of a Gascon swordsman: it is not coincidence that his family traces its source back to the same Basses-Pyrénées region of southern France. Here, the thin parched earth of this beautiful countryside bred fighters: olive cultivation gave the early Oliviers their name, and when his forbears, Protestants and clergymen, fled France in the late seventeenth century because of religious persecution, one found his way to England in the entourage of William of Orange. By his own father, Olivier was named after a sixteenth-century ancestor, Laurent Olivier. English to the core, a part of him still kept alive the swagger of this proud corner of France: no Englishman has the touchy and turbulent pride, the volatility, he shows in his acting. He has always been one of the élite guard defending his monarch and country: Athos, Porthos and Aramis were also Gascons.

Laurence Kerr Olivier was born on 22 May, 1907, at 5 am, in the London suburb of Dorking in Surrey. In 1926, not yet twenty, having been a student for less than two years at the Central School of Speech Training and Dramatic Art, he joined the Birmingham Repertory Theatre. Sixty years on he was still acting: in late 1986 he appeared on television in the serialisation of J. B. Priestley's *Lost Empires*, while his holographed head, as "Akash", activated nightly in the musical *Time* at London's Dominion Theatre, kept his name in lights over St Giles Circus as a "live" performer throughout that same year. But his last real stage role had been as John Tagg in Trevor Griffiths's *The Party* at the National Theatre twelve years before, while in between these landmarks, and as well as his numerous film performances, he had played a dozen or so major television roles which included Lear, Big Daddy in *Cat on a Hot Tin Roof* and Clifford Mortimer in *A Voyage Round my Father*.

Twenty years ago, in his introduction to a book, *Techniques of the Stage Fight*, by William Hobbs, Olivier made a list, without pausing for reflection, of the accidents suffered during his career:

1 broken ankle.
2 torn cartilages (1 perforce yielding to surgery).
2 broken calf muscles.
3 ruptured Achilles tendons.
Untold slashes including a full thrust razor-edged sword wound
    in the breast (thrilling).
Landing from considerable height, scrotum first, upon acrobat's
    knee.
Hanging by hand to piano wire forty feet up for some minutes
    (hours?) on account of unmoored rope.
Hurled to the stage from thirty feet due to faultily moored rope
    ladder.
Impalement upon jagged ply cut-outs.
Broken foot bone by standing preoccupied in camera track.
Broken face by horse galloping into camera while looking
    through finder.
Near broken neck diving into net.
Several shrewd throws from horses including one over beast's
    head into lake.
One arrow shot between shinbones.
Water on elbow.

Water pretty well everywhere.
Hands pretty well misshapen now through "taking" falls.
Quite a few pretended injuries while it was really gout.
Near electrocution through scimitar entering studio dimmer
   while backing away from unwelcome interview.
Etc, etc, etc . . .

There were many more that he could have included in this list (and
many since he made it). Although viewed in one way Olivier's
life has been solid, sometimes even frenetic, achievement – as one
or two contributors to this book describe, and the awesome
Chronology at the end only too starkly demonstrates – seen from
the opposite side the price paid has been dizzyingly high. In order
to provide a useful if very compressed chronological backbone to
what follows, I shall now endeavour to expand on Olivier's list
and place certain of these honourable scars in their proper sequence.

In fact, Olivier's first accident was in 1914 when he was only
seven. A horse and cart knocked him down in Buckingham Palace
Road. Five years later, when he was twelve, the biggest blow that
life could offer, struck him: his mother died of a brain tumour.
"Great suffering," he pronounced, "could often implant in some
mysterious way an unexpected strength." A remarkable father and
a good education ensured that he did survive, although "a shrimp
as a child and a weed as a youth" – arms hanging "like wires from
my shoulders" – he didn't at first look equipped for that career in
which the body was one of the main capital assets.

The French philosopher and playwright, Sartre, wrote in *Un
Théâtre de situations* that there was no such thing as an accident,
perhaps echoing Hamlet's "there is a special providence in the fall
of a sparrow". In Olivier's case the tempo of accidents seems to
have quickened from about 1925 onwards, when he plunged into
the footlights in a sketch called "Unfailing Instinct". This was
followed by: knocks from strike-breaking during the General
Strike with his friend Ralph Richardson; jaundice, caught in time
for a film called *The Yellow Ticket*; while the "broken ankle" that
heads the list resulted from a leap over a balcony in his first West
End lead (Bothwell in *Queen of Scots*, 1934).

His "Near broken neck" happened when, in the film of *Fire
Over England* (1937), he brought fire over himself, slipping on a
petrol-sprayed deck and crashing heavily into the safety net
stationed overboard. Badly executed falls and dives in the disas-

trous *Romeo* of 1939 produced the "misshapen hands". But athlete's foot (*Wuthering Heights*, 1939); smashed up training planes on runways (as Lieutenant RNVR, Worthy Down, Sussex, 1942); a damaged nerve in the ear from flying though a storm; a near miss from a cockpit fire on the night flight from Lisbon to London – all these showed him at the mercy of a destiny or force other than his own.

Henry V (1943) led him back to the true path of self-inflicted wounds and mutilations. When showing Irish Agincourt extras on the Ennis Kerry estate, County Wicklow, how to drop twenty feet from the bough of a tree in order to unhorse a French knight he cracked the right ankle (he underestimated the number of ankle injuries). Later he received the "Broken face" when he persuaded one rider to charge his viewfinder on the reasonable assumption that the horse would swerve off to avoid the solid iron camera unit – it didn't, and the viewfinder dealt a deep gash to lip and gum, as well as dislocating his shoulder.

I haven't been able to trace the scimitar entering the studio dimmer, unless he was referring, symbolically, to an odd incident he later recalled in another book when, after he played *Richard III* in Paris, Ralph Richardson entered his hotel room, gathered him in his arms like a baby and carried him to the edge of the balcony, sixty feet above the cobbled street, threatening to drop him. Near electrocution? "We were both very foolish," Richardson said the next day.

Art imitated real life, and for Hotspur he devised such a gory death—a huge chopping swipe of the sword by Prince Hal to sever the carotid artery—that many in the audience believed, from the sudden appearance of blood on his neck and the way in which he crashed to the floor, that Hal had mistimed his blow and really killed him. It was as the dandified Mr Puff, in *The Critic*, that Olivier had his biggest fright. Perched upon a plywood cloud (responsible for "the impalement upon jagged ply") he was swept up out of sight into the flies; one night one of the two piano wires holding the seat snapped at the forty foot apex of flight: after "some minutes (hours?)", astute tugging on the rope by a flyman drew him into the gallery, from where he slithered down, by means of a rope, to the stage. For good measure, on *The Critic's* last night in New York, doing his usual somersault on stage, he tore an Achilles tendon. The port wing of the airliner bringing him and Vivien Leigh home caught on fire, and the pilot had to crash-land on a tiny field in Connecticut.

The "full-thrust razor-edged sword" accident illustrates better than any other the unreliability of "the safer the more dangerous" maxim Olivier professed to hold on stage fights. Filming *Hamlet*, which he also directed, he instructed Terence Morgan, playing Laertes, to lunge straight at his heart, saying he would parry the blow. Morgan obeyed, but then was appalled to see his sword going through the lace shirt and into Olivier's chest: "He looked terribly surprised and glared at me." Olivier also described this accident as "thrilling". The Gascon speaks.

The gout ("Quite a few pretended injuries") appeared in his big toe when he set out on the Old Vic Antipodean Tour in 1948: "A burning pain like white hot needles." On the second night of *Richard III* in Sydney, in the fight with Richmond, he slipped, tearing the cartilage of his right knee. Injected with morphine he carried on playing the hunchback Gloucester using a period crutch; one subsequent night he broke the crutch, in rage, over the back of Brackenbury, and stage hands had to fashion a new end.

Perhaps this intensifying of accidents was a symptom of the impending break-up with his wife, Vivien Leigh: she didn't love him any more, she told him when the trip was over, and deadly competition between them took the place of love. Yet, three years later, in 1951, Jean-Louis Barrault, visiting London with his company and playing at the St James's Theatre, then under Olivier–Leigh management, observed, "Vivien and Larry formed a princely couple . . . We made acquaintance with one of the best theatre publics in the world: spontaneity, fundamental childhood, openness, human warmth." Barrault was not fooled for long by Vivien: later, directing her in Giraudoux's *Duel of Angels*, adapted by Christopher Fry, he noted that one thing really surprised him about her. "She worked on her part with a hatred for her character – in this case Paola. She assailed her. She was constantly on the lookout for reasons for not loving her. This forced me to plead for Paola. She attacked her by provoking antipathy. It was only when she had exhausted all the reasons for hating her that she assumed her."

Olivier's most dramatic flesh wound occurred during the filming of *Richard III* (1954) on location north of Madrid. George Brown, a master archer, loosed a warhead arrow which instead of lodging in the cork over his horse's flanks, pierced Olivier's fake rubber armour and stuck in the calf of his left leg ("between shinbones"). What did he do, but sit quite still on the horse with the arrow sticking out of his left leg until it was established that the sequence had been properly filmed, and how to achieve the transition to the next shot, before he said, "Get me off this horse and find me a doctor!" All control vanished a little while later when a Spanish stallion carrying the almost blind Esmond Knight into battle tried to mount his white mare. "Get this bloody horse out of my hair!" Olivier screamed.

By that time, at forty-seven, he had become a legend as a miraculous survivor: water "pretty well everywhere"; Achilles tendons popping like elastic bands. I have omitted other minor injuries: a torn calf-muscle here (*The Beggar's Opera*, 1952), a back stroked lightly by a stingray's tail there (at Noël Coward's, Blue Harbour, Jamaica). "It is a well known thing," he had blasted Richardson long before, driving his friend's little car at fifty miles an hour over the Croydon cross-roads when traffic lights didn't exist, "that when you get to a point of danger you must get over it as quickly as you can." Accident had created around him a cloak of comic inviolability. You can't have comedy without pain, and painful though the accidents were, he could always rise above them with defiant laughter.

Injuries now began to give way to illnesses, and they weren't funny. But I must curtail this list and refrain from details of the fatigue, disease, major, or minor, surgery that have been this actor's extraordinary and painful burden for the last two decades. Suffice it to say that he beat the family disease, cancer, which carried off mother, father, and elder brother; also pneumonia, thrombosis, labyrinthitis, dermato-poly-myocitis, etc, etc, etc . . . It is not surprising that in the many brilliant death scenes he has played recently in films and on television he has sometimes given the impression that, like the fox confronting its mortal enemy, he might be feigning death to escape death a little longer. In old age he has played d'Artagnan constantly.

How can Olivier's miraculous power of survival be explained? Try to portray him in Freudian terms and there isn't, possibly, that much to tell. The outline of the man is deceptively simple. Ego: the humble, or not-so-humble actor laddie. Super Ego: captain of the ship with an undying sense of service. Id: drinker, swearer, prankster, etc. Little is revealed, little done justice to by this approach. Freud's confidence trick has been to make us all believe that we are as afflicted as he was. Olivier definitely was not. Consider him as an escape artist, a survivor, and he at once achieves a quality of mystery and elusiveness.

One clue, perhaps, is to be found in the customs of primitive tribes. Just as primitive man thought that by hunting and killing an animal, then eating it, he absorbed its soul into his own, has Olivier, by mastering so many roles, come magically and spiritually to assume the life and power of all those he has played? For one who has lived and died so many times, fallen victim to the most deadly diseases, only to emerge, apparently unshaken and whole, on the other side, there would seem to be no rational explanation.

There is another possibility (and leaving aside his own determination, the excellent medical care, the love of family and friends). Interwoven with the many accidents and illnesses is the amazing, teeming life Olivier has been portraying all the while, the myriad forms, the transformations, the different disguises he has donned, the different deceptions he has practised. His parts, finally, have exorcised his illnesses: consider how he triumphed, after a long succession of them, with his towering portrayal of James Tyrone in *Long Day's Journey Into Night*. He has never become dead, never adult in the way of someone who protects himself in his shell: illnesses have been, viewed in one way, the shells of rigidity he has thrown off. The surprised, curious gleam of the boy has remained always in his eye.

So his parts have kept him moving forward. They have swallowed him and not he them: he has found self-confirmation in becoming others, not the other way about. This way he has avoided play-acting in life. Considered in relation to his service to acting, these accidents, later illnesses, come to be seen, perhaps, as no more than incidental – a minor penalty imposed each time he had made his exit from one metamorphosis and assumed the next.

The contributors to this book are primarily concerned with the fertile and abundant life which Olivier has created over sixty years on stage, on film, and on television. They are friends, colleagues, young and old – and some critics – with Sheridan Morley on what Olivier thought of critics and they of him. As much as any other man or woman this century Olivier has become part of everyone's private world. There exists no outstanding and complete biography – for all the numerous accounts of him that have been written – for the simple reason that the total of the man, his life and his work, is still too great to be embraced by any one individual. As Mark Amory, who contributes his experiences with Olivier "The Author", wrote in a *Spectator* review some time ago, "After fourteen books, Olivier remains a fascinating subject," yet, "the first difficulty is that he seems less than his parts". Even Olivier himself "casts light but does not explain".

Here, instead, I offer a different kind of Life: twenty-two short biographies – twenty-three if we include Antony Sher's jacket drawing. Each reveals a sharp and private perception, some of them not recognisably of the same person.

I asked each contributor to concentrate on a certain aspect or area of the subject, so that the pieces could be arranged in three sections. The first, "The Actor", includes what might be called the well-dressed pieces; the second, "The Director", shows the subject slightly more déshabillé. The last, "The Man", carries the reader, I venture to hope, further into the mystery and elusiveness of this great actor.

I have also tried to make this celebration a little different from the usual *Festschrift* by encouraging contributors to be frank and honest. This approach is, I am happy to report, confirmed by the subject himself in a story that John Mortimer tells at the beginning of the final piece. I will not lift Olivier's remarks out of context, but they are my authority for this book, and for all biographical writing. Honesty is the sincerest form of flattery, truth the greatest form of celebration.

But I never did discover where the landing, in Olivier's list, "scrotum first, upon acrobat's knee", was from. Any ideas?

PART ONE
THE ACTOR

Richard III, New Theatre, London, 1949.
Drawing by Griff.

PEGGY ASHCROFT

PEGGY ASHCROFT

Peggy Ashcroft (b. 1907) is one of the most beloved and admired members of her profession. An actress of outstanding integrity she is alert to new playwrights as well as serving the classics with a rare judgement, versatility, and skill. Since she was created a DBE in 1956 she has been awarded honorary degrees by eight universities, and she is the first British actress to have a theatre named after her in her own lifetime, in Croydon where she was born. She has known Olivier for over sixty years.

SALAD DAYS

One early autumn, in a bygone age, when life and prospects were so fresh at the beginning of a term that the end of a year seemed like the beginning of a new one – two young people entered, separately, the Albert Hall. They were starting their lives as an actor and actress at the Central School of Speech Training and Dramatic Art – Larry aged seventeen and myself sixteen-and-a-half. He was one of the élite – one of five male students – she one of the herd of eighty female students! Probably we didn't speak for many weeks – I have no recollection. But he leaves an indelible picture – dark hair standing on end, heavy eyebrows, seeming almost one rather than two, but eyes the same as now and unlike anyone else's.

Myths, of course, were built about the five men – one was about George Coulouris,* overwhelmingly Greek, who, it was rumoured, kept a knife down his sock! The Larry myth, perhaps because he seemed a fairly scrawny figure, with wrists well protruding from threadbare cuffs, was that he walked shoeless across the park each day in order to save his shoe-leather! I see him as clearly then as I do in so many later stages and performances. The explosive energy, a certain eccentricity of very precise enunciation, the dynamic vigour and the fun were all there.

---

* George Coulouris (b. 1903). Actor, worked mostly in the United States in 1930s and 1940s (including Orson Welles' *Citizen Kane*). Returned to Britain in 1950 in mainly character parts.

As students our paths only crossed on two occasions – one in our first year when we were paired together in a dialogue competition as Mr and Mrs Inkpen – heavy with jokes of Mr and Mrs Pen and Ink. We each won a silver cup for that! The second event was our end of term public show. We appeared in the trial scene from *The Merchant of Venice* – our Judge Athene Seyler★ – and each won a gold medal for playing Shylock and the clerk of the court. (Larry is convinced he never received his, but mine is still in my possession.)

So ended our school days. Larry forged ahead – I remember seeing him early on as Malcolm in a rather bad production of *Macbeth* at the Royal Court. I remember little about it – but I will never forget anything about his performance of *Macbeth* at Stratford in 1954.

Post-school period – we were both cast in a John Drinkwater play *Bird in Hand* at the Birmingham Repertory Theatre – but not included in the regular season; memorable chiefly for a visit to Stratford-upon-Avon with John Drinkwater where we saw *Antony and Cleopatra* at the local cinema, the theatre having just been burnt down; and we were taken to a magical dinner at Hall's Croft which then belonged to an American friend of John Drinkwater.

Romance? No – only in retrospect . . . many years later Larry told me that when we went to tea with a member of the Rep. Co. in his digs in Birmingham and our host had retired to the lavatory, the sudden pulling of the chain prevented him from proposing! The company dispersed – the opportunity never recurred!

And our final association alas, our professional partnership brief but our friendship lasting – was in the 1935 *Romeo and Juliet* at the New Theatre. A glorious occasion and one of John Gielgud's finest productions, in which he gave a superb Mercutio before exchanging with Larry as Romeo. But to me Larry's was the definitive Romeo – gauchely graceful, awkward, ardent – a complete characterisation of an impulsive adolescent.

At twenty-eight and twenty-nine we set our sights on a sixteen and fourteen-year-old Romeo and Juliet and John Gielgud's fast moving production never called into question those children's inevitable fate in the mesh of the Capulet–Montague hatred. That

---

★ Athene Seyler (b. 1889). Herself a Gold Medalist (at the Royal Academy of Dramatic Art, 1908), she went on "to specialise in comedy acting". Her second husband, Nicholas Hannen, was a member of Olivier's New Theatre company.

Larry's Romeo was denigrated by every critic but one – St John Ervine – was proof of their blindness to the challenging and original road he was taking, and was to make his own, in the classics. Happy Days indeed!

J.C. TREWIN

J. C. TREWIN

J. C. Trewin (b. 1908) doyen of practising drama critics, has been covering the London stage through more than fifty years (forty of them for the *Illustrated London News*). A former literary editor of the *Observer*, he has written a great many books on the theatre. He received the OBE in 1981, is a Fellow of the Royal Society of Literature, and holds an honorary degree from Birmingham University.

GIVING
THE COUNTERSIGN

There has never been, I think, an English repertory theatre quite
like Barry Jackson's, hidden modestly behind New Street Station
in Birmingham. The building is visible still, more than seventy
years old and used today as a thriving drama school (the modern
"Rep" is elsewhere). Even to walk along Station Street, uninspiring
in itself, is to move through theatre history. It was here that
Jackson, then aged thirty-three, a wealthy man and a lavish poten-
tial patron of the stage, expressed what lay behind his hobby when
he spoke, rather bashfully, on a February night in 1913, the rhymed
iambics of John Drinkwater's prologue, "We have the challenge
of the mighty line, / God grant us grace to give the countersign."

There, during the winter of 1926, an actor of nineteen, Laurence
Olivier, virile, heavy-browed, darkly handsome in an Italianate
mode, was appearing at what had become in effect a national
theatre in a Midland city; often it could draw visitors from London.
Jackson had built an auditorium, holding nearly 500, in steeply
raked steps. There was an apron stage; everywhere, plenty of
space. Neither players nor audience would cower in the dimmer
crevices. Those were days elsewhere of brave but desperate
weekly-change repertory, of fighting the more or less impossible;
thus, at Plymouth within ten years or so, I saw 500 plays upon a
stage like a tilted tea-tray perched upon a hidden spiral staircase.

Barry Jackson at that time would have runs of three weeks or a month – as a minor poet would say, he "set the fires ablaze in Station Street" – and his Birmingham company, usually (though not always) with a challenging programme, ensured that excitement would be contagious.

Certainly Laurence Olivier looked for excitement. It is a repertory audience's privilege to watch an actor grow; Olivier responded, even if, very early, his sense of mischief might have toppled him during a trivial curtain-raiser by Eden Phillpotts, part of a double bill. (The Devonian Phillpotts, who wrote *The Farmer's Wife*, was one of the Repertory's mascot-dramatists.) Surprised by a burglar at a house-party, a youth of the day, predictably monocled and drawling, should have replied to the intruder's sharp "Who are you?" with a haughty "We are Conservatives." On the last night, to his director's horror – this director was the Irishman W. G. Fay – and to the audience's pleasure, he said "We're Freemasons, Frothblowers, and Gugnuncs," a sentence of transient topicalities which had the house in uproar.

A sulphurous offstage interview followed. Olivier survived and went on to play such a part as Parolles, presented (to the approval of Bernard Shaw, in one of the audiences) as an amiable, too smart man-about-Paris, a *sommelier*'s scourge, in a modern-dress *All's Well That Ends Well*. That was at the zenith of the modern-dress vogue which Jackson, oddly for him, had been encouraging. The young actor was also Tony Lumpkin in *She Stoops to Conquer* and, most surprisingly, Uncle Vanya (a long time yet before a celebrated Astrov in the same play). He believed already, and showed it, that the kindling of excitement should be an actor's essential task. He sought, as he did invariably, to grasp the house from his first entrance: downright, unconcealed acting, by no means the thing during the 1920s when, as with Hawtrey and, especially, with Gerald du Maurier, naturalism ruled: a player had to adapt his technique to the throw-away method which was dangerous unless judged by a master, and often difficult then. The young Olivier would never have joined the club. He spoke "bold, and forth on". Certainly he did so when Jackson brought him to London for the Royal Court season of 1928. A modern-dress *Macbeth*, never more than a doomed experiment as Jackson acknowledged on the first night, had to sag: the Macbeth, Eric Maturin, a good drawing-room man, was no Shakespearian ("upon this *blasted* heath" he said as a matter of course). But, in the circumstances, Olivier did all that could have been done with Malcolm, in dressing-gown or kilt, and the critics agreed.

He was in a *Back to Methuselah* revival – the pentateuch had been a Birmingham triumph five years before – and he appeared also, and remarkably, as the hero in a resurrection of Tennyson's forgotten verse-drama, *Harold*: "Here rose the dragon-banner of our realm, / Here fought, here fell, our Norman-slander'd King." Better than its reputation for tushery, if seldom in sight of the mighty line – nobody now will rescue it from a bottom shelf – *Harold* had very few supporters in the empty spaces of the Court. Still, though scarcely yet a governing figure, Olivier could spark off Saxon fire. Again, his primary task was to excite. People who watched him in these days and through years ahead, knew he was someone who tried to ignite the imagination even when a part was as pale as the lover in Drinkwater's gentle comedy of *Bird in Hand*. He acted the youth for some months at the old Royalty in Dean Street, Soho, during the summer and autumn of 1928, with his later first wife, Jill Esmond Moore,* as the girl Peggy Ashcroft had created in Birmingham.

*　　*　　*

Thenceforward he would gradually burnish his name in the usual complex mosaic of West End plays – this and that, mostly obscure now – with periods in New York and Hollywood. It is unprofitable to guess what could have happened if, after a Sunday night when he created Captain Stanhope in Sherriff's war-play, *Journey's End* – a front-line dug-out before St Quentin during March 1918 – he had gone on to a sustained run instead of taking the transient *Beau Geste* in a version of P. C. Wren's Foreign Legion novel. But everyone talked about *Beau Geste*, too unwarily; Basil Dean was directing; and an actor at that point could hardly have chosen otherwise. A catalogue of the opening years of the 1930s is unhelpful. We can remember, perhaps, that in Noël Coward's *Private Lives*, Olivier was the first Victor Prynne, one of what he called the "wretched pair of other parts", a character like a slow-moving full-back baffled by an electric eel (Coward himself) at wing three-quarter. Strange casting, it may seem now, but Olivier would go on to play Victor in New York.

* They married in 1930, had one son, Tarquin, and divorced in 1940.

His stern challenge in the mid-1930s was the invitation by John Gielgud, first Shakespearian of the age, to alternate Romeo and Mercutio at the New Theatre. Not an approved verse-speaker, he had to open for six weeks as Romeo, facing cruel comparison with Gielgud's Mercutio whose Queen Mab aria ("Her whip, of cricket's bone; the lash of film") was expressed so subtly that it could be nearly impossible to replay it in the mind. It had become modish to blame Olivier for staccato delivery and dry tone – criticism not altogether relaxed when the actors changed over – yet I can bring back the excitement, the gasp in the theatre, as his Romeo, olive-skinned, impetuous adolescent, never a disembodied lyric, entered straight from the high Renaissance, the scorch of the Veronese noonday, a world of hot sun, sharp swords, and brief lives. Some phrases, "Look, love, what envious streaks/ Do lace the severing clouds in yonder east," he caressed unforgettably. I thought then, and have continued to think, that it could be tiresome, Dogberry-minded indeed, to compare in detail actors who conquered in ways far different; but, at that hour, comparison was swamping.

For all that, it was fairly obvious, in the Shakespearian climate of the decade, that Olivier would go across to the Old Vic. An interregnum included the brief West End run of an attempt to approach an allegorical-political satire in terms of farcical comedy, J. B. Priestley's *Bees on the Boatdeck* of which nothing has been heard since. One can be sorry to have missed an entirely idiotic passage at the end of the last act when, as caretakers, the chief engineer (Ralph Richardson) and the second officer (Olivier) of a tramp steamer laid up in the backwater of a southern estuary, went into full-scale craziness for the benefit of a large, slow police-sergeant.

At last Olivier reached the Old Vic early in 1937, the old building awash with legend, Tyrone Guthrie* as director, Lilian Baylis† in her curtained box, and the gallery feverishly in waiting. He opened with a full-length Hamlet, boldest of choices, for no actor could be less plausibly the Hamlet of indecision; from the beginning, as Ivor Brown said in a first-night notice and many echoed him, this would be the flash-and-outbreak of a fiery mind. Far fewer people

* Tyrone Guthrie (1900–71), director. Important influence in the theatre both in England and the USA.
† Lilian Baylis (1874–1937), founder of the Old Vic and Sadler's Wells companies.

were suggesting now that Olivier had any trouble with verse.

He had, it emerged later, a hidden problem. Tyrone Guthrie had been impressed, as Olivier was himself – superfluously, it appeared – by the notion of a leading psychologist, Dr Ernest Jones, that Hamlet was a victim of the Oedipus complex, in love with his mother, a small matter that might explain a lot if it could be made clear. Scarcely anybody noticed. All that counted – and once more the phrase recurs – was the sheer excitement of the occasion: not an expected Hamlet but one that brought the generous Vic audience, cheering, to its feet, after Olivier, probably as athletic a Hamlet as any on record, had spent the night springing like a chamois across Guthrie's piled rostrums, an Alpine range. (Dorothy Dix, the gallant Queen, had to deal with a fantastic backward fall from one of these peaks at the end of the play). Whenever I could get away from Fleet Street on those *Hamlet* evenings, and happily it was often, I would hurry across to Waterloo Road where performances grew progressively more exciting, though one did feel – absurdly, perhaps – that maybe they ought not to have been exciting in this particular manner. Invariably, Olivier left in the mind the inexorable throbbing of the fourth-act soliloquy, "I do not know/ Why yet I live to say This thing's to do." James Agate said that the lines were "trumpet-moaned".

Olivier followed this with Sir Toby Belch in *Twelfth Night*, visually a compound of wiggery and nose-paste and acted like an elderly Skye terrier, ears pricked for mischief. (At any moment Toby might have slid into the "Frothblowers and Gugnuncs" of an earlier decade.) Later, in a production for Coronation year, his Henry V, coming from a grove of banners, was happiest in the wooing of Princess Katherine. Guthrie had insisted on the national paladin; but, beside the film that was still years in the distance, the Vic production would have seemed muted; in memory it does so now.

Presently, at the invitation of the Danish Tourist Board, Olivier returned to Hamlet, and at Elsinore itself, upon a platform in the vast castle courtyard of Kronborg. The company was variously changed: Vivien Leigh took over Ophelia from Cherry Cottrell, and Leo Genn from the curiously-cast Robert Newton as Horatio. There was much rehearsal, often in a glum drizzle – "Is there not rain enough in the sweet heavens?" was a popular line – but today the production is remembered less for the courtyard performances before the honeycombed grey-and-silver northern wall, than for the première on a night when the weather made any kind of open-air work out of the question.

Hour by hour rain swept across the Kattegat from Sweden. "This must stop!" said Lilian Baylis. Even she could do nothing; early in the evening Guthrie resolved to take a chance and to allow a performance, Olivier in control, to be improvised in the ballroom of the Marienlyst hotel not far from the castle. The seven or eight critics who had travelled from London were enlisted to range hundreds of gilt chairs (according to Guthrie, 870 of them) in a wide semi-circle. When we had done this, and the ballroom was crammed, a Danish Prince and Princess in the front row, rain still hammering against the windows, *Hamlet* began, among and round the audience and upon the craftily employed splinter of a cabaret stage. It proved to be astonishingly dramatic, the players' technique responsive to any emergency. Olivier was, in essence, his Hamlet from the Vic, but that night it did appear to some of us that he had never acted with so much relishing invention that he may hardly have noticed himself in the surge of events. We realised, too, on that single Marienlyst night that the proscenium stage was not sovereign: from this moment Guthrie decided to turn, as far as possible, from picture-frame Shakespeare to arena, open-stage, direction.

★   ★   ★

Back in Waterloo Road that autumn there would be a drop in tension. A heavily stylised *Macbeth*, directed by Michel Saint-Denis,* would hardly have prepared us for Olivier's Stratford achievement of eighteen years ahead: it arrived, too, at the hour of Lilian Baylis's death which petrified the theatre she had ruled for a quarter of a century.

During the spring of 1938 Olivier's Iago, to the Othello of Ralph Richardson, suffered sadly from the still obliging Dr Jones's determined psychological speculation. He held now that Iago was subconsciously in love with Othello, "the homosexual foundation of which he did not understand": a hidden amour of which

* Michel Saint-Denis (1897–1971), influential French teacher and director who worked in England, and was joint founder of the Old Vic theatre school. During the second world war, as M. Duchesne, was the BBC's French expert and translator.

Richardson – not, in any event, surely cast – neither knew anything nor wished to know. In consequence, the night was fatally lop-sided. An ambitious play by James Bridie, *The King of Nowhere*, made disappointingly little effect. It was the portrait of an actor, vain and mentally unbalanced, cast suddenly for dictatorship. The time (Munich year) was awkward for such a part as this, though, at least, one can summon now Olivier's swoop and fury as the paranoic Vivaldi (somebody quoted Emily Brontë's "purple dress jagged with white lightnings"), and we may wonder how the piece might revive at a long remove from the fading thirties.

In the Vic's classical history this would be the time of Olivier's first Coriolanus (directed by Lewis Casson), a pillar of fire on a plinth of marble: we cannot hazard what Dr Johnson, who regarded the tragedy as "one of the most amusing of our author's perform-ances", might have said. One can hear yet the flint-flashed snap of "The word is *mildly*," the sound of the straight-flung revelation at Antium, and the voice, its noble baritone turned to an ice-bladed sickle, in the last defiance, "Cut me to pieces, Volsces!" before a tremendous death-fall. Sybil Thorndike, in Volumnia's suppli-cation, was marmoreal Rome personified.

The war went by, nearly to its final year. Then, after his service in the RNVR and the making of the *Henry V* film, Olivier reached that extraordinary period at the New Theatre (since rechristened the Albery in honour of the late Sir Bronson Albery) that should have a separate chapter in any history of the twentieth-century stage. In the thirties the New had meant Gielgud and many of his renowned parts; Olivier, besides alternating Romeo and Mercutio there, had been Bothwell in Gielgud's production of "Gordon Daviot's" *Queen of Scots*. In the autumn of 1944 the New kept its fame. The Old Vic company, Guthrie as administrator, would be in charge of a triumvirate, Olivier, Richardson, and a young director, John Burrell, practically all of whose work had been with the BBC. Sybil Thorndike, Joyce Redman, Margaret Leighton, Nicholas Hannen, George Relph, Harcourt Williams, were all in the cast. The collective name could have been the Theatre of Excitement.

*   *   *

Everything began with Guthrie's treatment of Ibsen's *Peer Gynt*, Richardson as Peer, in which Olivier subdued himself to the uncanny, chilling radiance of the Button Moulder with his few late entrances, a part that, in the thirties, Ion Swinley, grandly voiced and fated might-have-been of the classical theatre, had acted at the Vic. Next, Burrell's production of Shaw's *Arms and the Man*, guying fancy-dress heroics, Richardson as the "chocolate-cream soldier", and Olivier, though he did not like the part, able with comic bravura to pink Sergius Saranoff, the Ruritanian major whose forbears include Byron and Ouida, and who observes "This hand is more accustomed to the sword than the pen."

Presently, on September 13, 1944, I sat at the première that, possibly of all others in my stage experience, I value most – the *Richard III* when, in Shakespeare's Saturday-night melodrama, Olivier strode across the contentions of York and Lancaster to give the most theatrically overwhelming performance of the day: dominant from the moment he turned to move slowly downstage, pallid, evilly debonair, the man's deformity unexaggerated, the ends of his lank black hair flicked with red, his gait like a limping panther. Now, after a tensely held pause, he took the house into his confidence, beginning in tones thinly terrifying that some did not hesitate to call Irvingesque, "Now is the winter of our discontent." The speech was a blend that contained the passage from the second scene of the third act of *Henry VI, Part III* in which Richard of Gloucester boasts "I can . . . set the murderous Machiavel to school," a phrase Olivier pointed with an insolent zest and a sudden outflung, down-thrust gesture. From the first he preserved the man's unholy magnetism and his pride – this Plantagenet was not simply a night's exhibitionist; he was bred in that aery in the cedar's top. He had a glittering irony; in rage he could terrify ("Out on you, owls! Nothing but songs of death!"), and his silences, mocking or malign, were infinitely charged.

Too often other players of Richard had offered the mask without the mind, an animated oleograph to whom we responded simply, "Begin, murderer, leave thy damnable faces and begin." Not so here in a marriage of cold reason and forked-lightning: the true double Gloucester, mind and mask. Olivier never counterfeited the deep tragedian of the ponderous and marble jaws. His speech, flexible and swift, often mill-race swift, was bred of a racing brain. A few other players – particularly Baliol Holloway; less so, Donald Wolfit – had developed the Red King with a theatrical imagination; none had kept us so conscious of the usurper's intellect, made so persuasive every move on the board. Playgoers a generation hence would hear of the *diablerie*; the crackling sardonic humours; the imperatively regal gesture to Buckingham with which Richard proclaimed his new-born royalty in the moment of birth after the charade at Baynard's Castle; the figure, crowned and sceptred, that crouched upon the throne like some emanation from a witch's cauldron; the lunge back to the throne at "Is the chair empty? Is the sword unsway'd?"; the strangled sobbing of "There is no creature loves me"; the half-wistful, despairing "Not shine today!" as Richard studied the sky on the morning of Bosworth; and the doom in the distorted face, the prolonged spasm of the death agony before Richmond. It was a diabolical figure, so exciting in development that others in the cast were taken for granted (as well as a note in the first programme which explained usefully that Richmond would be "King Edward the Seventh").

There could not have been more of a swerve than from the Red King to Astrov, the meditative doctor of Chekhov's *Uncle Vanya*, that picture of frustration in the deep south of Russia at the ebb of the nineteenth century. John Burrell had succeeded with Shavian comedy and with the outline of *Richard III*. Now he preferred his Chekhov in slow motion. The revival needed itself to be revived, though individually the players (Richardson's Vanya, Margaret Leighton's Yelena) could command; and Olivier found in Astrov, doctor in permanent exile, a part he would repeat nearly twenty years on: the man who has what Vanya lacks, a redeeming passion, a deep-planted love for the kingdom of the trees. Olivier expressed him precisely in the quiet absorption of the speech over the chart: "And almost everything has gone, and nothing has been created to take its place."

It was improbable that the ensuing season, 1945–6, would match the first, but it did, opening with the great twin brethren, Burrell's production of the two Parts of *Henry IV*, Richardson's Falstaff acutely idiosyncratic and unvulgarised. Olivier enjoyed the virtuosity of moving on consecutive nights from Hotspur to Shallow. As Hotspur, no simple romantic blazon but hurtling, uncouth, passionate, he was yet the light by which the chivalry of England moved. The stammer that had been traditional, though only through thirty years, had derived from a dubious reading of Lady Percy's line in *Part Two*, "speaking thick which nature made his blemish." ("Thick" more reasonably implied "thick and fast".) Wisely, Olivier would not let tradition cloud him; he turned it to advantage by stammering only on the letter "w", so that when

Hotspur received his mortal wound he stood momentarily before he fell, his last word struggling for utterance:

> . . . No, Percy, thou art dust
> And food for –
> *Prince Hal*: For worms, brave Percy; fare thee well, great heart.

In *Part Two* Olivier's Shallow, carefully, maybe too carefully, composed, did give a clear gleam from the old man's inch of taper as he sat, faintly babbling during the silver night-piece on Cotswold, wine and leather-coats upon the orchard table, Miles Malleson's Silence jetting into song, and Falstaff looking on, contemplative.

He would have three other parts during those historic years: none so startling as the night when he elected to follow his Oedipus in Yeats's plain-text version of Sophocles (suggested by Guthrie) with, of all things, Sheridan's Puff in *The Critic*. This offended some people, among them Guthrie who left the production of *Oedipus* to Saint-Denis. Even so, the night was prized by many who admired both the sculptural quality of the self-blinded King with his shattering cry of anguish, and the "practitioner in panegyric", a dapper elf, his nose tip-tilted, who during a last pantomime rally in Malleson's production, soared to heaven on a wave and descended on a cloud. Something like that, anyway. The charting of the manoeuvre is complicated; in action it would be dangerous.

Olivier's last part at this meridian of the Vic would be Lear in a revival (1946) when his performance outshone his own production. He rose with the play from the early cunning hint of senility, enough to show that royal Lear was on the edge, to the ultimate entry with Cordelia in his arms and the echoing quadruple "Howl!" He was less well received than he might have been (Ivor Brown was among his chief supporters), possibly because it was too soon after the acclamation for Donald Wolfit's Lear which, for me, in spite of its nobility, suffered from a creeping monotony of intonation. Re-living the New Theatre night after forty years, I am apt now to concentrate on Alec Guinness's Fool. The part is neither prancing jester nor piping grotesque, and Guinness, wry, quiet, true, with a dog's devotion, restored it to its proper place.

One postscript. After two years Olivier returned to the New – with Vivien Leigh, his second wife – from the Vic company's long tour of Australasia. From that spring of 1949 I bring back now neither an exact Sir Peter Teazle nor the Chorus in Anouilh's *Antigone*, but once more Olivier's *Richard III*. "Anybody," I said then, "who writes the word 'great' must do so with a cautious half-glance over his shoulder. But here there is no reason on earth to hedge. Again this Richard, one rais'd in blood and one in blood establish'd, is knave, King and ace." Yet again then, and for history, the Theatre of Excitement.

FABIA DRAKE

FABIA DRAKE

Fabia Drake has been an actress for as long as anyone can remember: she became the youngest student ever to attend the Royal Academy of Dramatic Art. In her late teens she played in the West End – notably with Marie Tempest – and in plays by John Galsworthy, Aldous Huxley and St John Ervine. Then, aged twenty-five, she began a career as a Shakespearian player. Recently she was in *The Jewel in the Crown* for Granada, and played the part of Catherine Alan in the film of *A Room with a View*.

FABIANA VIOLACEA

I write as Laurence Olivier's oldest friend, one who has known him since he was ten years old. A seventy-year-old photograph still exists which reveals us playing together in the Kitchen Scene from *Twelfth Night*. Only he is playing Maria, and I am playing Sir Toby Belch which he has described as "a performance for which the casting must forever be regarded as the most unique in all theatre history".

At that time I was the only person they could find who was small enough to join the select band of choristers from All Saints', Margaret Street, London, when one of their members – the one due to play Sir Toby – was taken ill on the afternoon of the first performance. Likewise I was the only juvenile member of the All Saints' congregation already pursuing a stage career, although I was still in the initial stage of training at the Academy of Dramatic Art (later RADA). This had accepted me at the age of nine. Many years later, in 1978, I published an autobiography, *Blind Fortune*. Laurence Olivier wrote a most endearing Foreword, in which he said:

> I am probably Fabby's oldest friend – the pet-name was picked up from her father, a churchwarden where I was in the choir and she a devout communicant – and I very much share with her her enthusiasm for what Ellen Terry said about acting and religion. Which was; "You cannot act without a feeling for religion".

I am aware of much religious feeling, but no certain belief. I first knew Fabby when she was helping her father (a brilliant ballroom-dancer, heavy, but light as a feather on his feet) to prepare our little Choir school for a Christmas Fancy Dress Ball. The Treble voice ranged from nine to fourteen. I was ten, so I was quite late on in my turn to be taken, one by one, through the waltz steps by Fabby, who disguised what must have been her growing sense of tedium pretty successfully but I was getting apprehensive enough to watch the others very closely and sort of dance the basis of the waltz to myself.

I felt a certain emotion as she took my hands. If she was aware of this she did nothing to show it. Simultaneously to both of us it must have been apparent that she was a Princess out of my star. Certainly she was twelve – maybe even thirteen – and she acted more grown up still.

Ten and twelve years old, then. An early start to what was to become, later on, a deep friendship. He touchingly paid tribute to this in a letter he wrote to me in April, 1981, which contained the following words:

My darling, I have planted a special plant in loving recognition of our beautiful friendship. It is called a "Fabiana Violacea". One of the books describes it as "of a heath-like character", but the flowers are tubular and of a rich blue-mauve. I hope you like the sound of it. I cannot wait for the first flowering it puts forth.

But it is as an actor that I would like to write of him, for the line that he spoke at the Memorial Service to his lifelong friend, Ralph Richardson, "we shall not look upon his like again" applies so appositely to this man himself. Someone who has grown up under the impetus of his inspiration – as of a great lodestar shining from the viewpoint of a player.

It is important that those of us who have lived through the reign of Olivier in the kingdom of our theatre should recognise what that reign has achieved. He has widened the frontiers of playing. To class him as a great actor is not enough; he is a player who has exercised a galvanising effort throughout his career and on every stage upon which he has played. I will try to assess his impact in some of the greatest of these performances.

The first went unrecognised by nearly everyone who wrote

about acting at that time. When Olivier played Romeo in October, 1935, at the New Theatre (Gielgud was Mercutio, and after six weeks they exchanged parts), he received notices of such blistering scorn that he was almost unable to appear on the second night and offered to resign. I had seen his Dress Rehearsal (I was myself playing in *Lady Precious Stream* at the time of the first night) and I had been overwhelmed by the magic of his rendering. At a distance of over fifty years I can still hear the astonishing recognition of first love that came from the two words that he uttered under Juliet's balcony when she calls him back – when he says "My dear . . ." Two words, two unimportant little words, "My dear". How was it possible to invest in them the whole story of a love that will surpass death, of a love that is greater than life? It is inconceivable that the dramatic critics of the daily papers who sat and watched the revelation that Olivier was giving to the part of Romeo could not recognise what was happening before their very eyes; the part was being reborn. It was not only the Balcony Scene; there is a later scene called the "Banishment Scene", Scene 3, Act III, which is where all the Romeos I had seen previously – and often since – had come, as Shakespeare himself says in Hamlet's Advice to the Players, had come "tardy off". Because the Banishment Scene is a colossal outburst of agony, it needs colossal playing . . . Yet the critic of the *Evening News* that came out the next day delivered his verdict thus:– "A delicate Juliet but a ranting Romeo". Ranting? That unbearable agony . . . *ranting*?

When I read this afternoon publication after the horrors of the morning papers I seized my telephone and rang the brilliant, the beloved, the blessed Romeo to tell him that there were other people who were closer to the truth about playing than those who wrote about it from an alien, an outside viewpoint and that, for them, this was by far the greatest Romeo ever to have been seen. The following letter (unexpectedly preserved and only just resurfaced) came from the New Theatre on October 19th:

Fabbie, my precious,
    First of all to thank you once more for the lovely black swan and the beautiful telegram but mainly for all your angelic solicitations throughout this trying time. You really are an angel to write me that lovely letter. They were horrible, weren't they? But I'm ever so much cheered now and feel much better for everyone going out of their way to be so kind and you in

45

particular, my darling. I must admit to a slight increase of pulse since Mr Agate yesterday* and I hear he was even better on the wireless tonight. I am writing this in between the "farewell" and Mantua and I'm afraid giving a lousy performance tonight on account of a bad cold and general reaction. Let's hope I'm better when you're there tomorrow, it won't be for want of trying if not!

All my love and gratitude, darling. See you tomorrow, I hope.

It should encourage all stumbling actors as they grope their way towards the stars to learn that the greatest of them was not only unacknowledged but badly bludgeoned when he laid his first trail of glory.

Romeo was the beginning.

Later came *Richard III* . . . what a world lies between them! We are back at the New Theatre and yet another page of theatrical history is being written, one, now, that is more widely known. But the impact of a live performance upon a live audience is so infinitely much greater than the subsequent film version of the same play became, that, once again, it becomes necessary to try to recapture something of that impact.

This started, of course, with the very first, the crucial opening soliloquy. One recognised the actual presence of evil immediately. This from the Anglo-Catholic choirboy of All Saints', Margaret Street, from the son of a dedicated priest, from a man to whom religion has always been a deep, intuitive awareness. It came upon me – afterwards – as an astonishing revelation of the extent of Laurence Olivier's acting genius. During the performance he did not exist. All that was there was the Crookback, the deeply dangerous devil, and, that night, trying afterwards to sleep, I remained haunted by what I had seen.

Thus it is to surrender to the power of the mind generated by one man's impersonation of someone other than himself.

Coriolanus comes next in my memory. So startling was this performance that, ever since, I have written to my friend as "Larioli" echoing the "Corioli" of that text.

Perhaps many people who saw this performance will stay with the memory of the astounding, astonishing death-fall that Olivier

* See p. 90 below.

contrived at the end of the play. Falling forward, head first, from an upper rostrum where, somehow, his ankles were held and he was prevented from killing himself literally – and nightly!

Here it may be timely to mention the bodily pressures to which Olivier has always been willing to subject himself.

I know of no other living actor who has been able to combine this physical fearlessness with such a rigorously trained body: the hours he has spent in the gym can only be guessed at. He writes of it himself when he writes of "bodily expression balanced by a technique that could control all physical expressiveness from dead stillness to an almost acrobatic agility."

I believe this faculty in acting – which he alone seems to possess today – was an actual element in the equipment of the players of the Elizabethan theatre when it was called "activity".

And Harold Hobson also went back to those Elizabethans when, describing Olivier's Macbeth at Stratford-upon-Avon in 1954, he wrote in the *Sunday Times*: "The greatest 'Macbeth' since 'Macbeth'."

This brings us to what many people consider to have been Olivier's finest achievement as an actor. His Macbeth in *Macbeth*.

Astonishingly he had played the part before, in 1937, and he had failed. This he confirms in his autobiography where he tells how Noël Coward "nearly died laughing when he came to see it". But then he had had (a) the wrong director, Michel Saint-Denis, instead of the infinitely sensitive and intuitive Glen Byam Shaw★ who was a great director of Shakespeare. He had also (b) the wrong Lady Macbeth, the American Judith Anderson, instead of the sinuous, snake-like brilliance of his second wife, Vivien Leigh, who was the best Lady Macbeth I have ever seen. She did indeed "look like the innocent flower" and became "the serpent under't". As he became the only Macbeth.

Yet I had come out in the middle of the Saint-Denis production, my allegiance to Olivier, the actor, being too great to go on watching him being *impeded*. Now he was nearly twenty years older and his own understanding had been enormously increased by the slings and arrows of outrageous fortune that he was suffering at that time. An actor is great or greater according to the extent

★ Glen Byam Shaw (b. 1904) actor, and later director. Director of the Shakespeare Memorial Theatre at Stratford-upon-Avon in the 1950s. Married to Angela Baddeley (1904–76).

of his understanding of all humanity, and what happens to him in his own life will increase or not increase this understanding.

No one I have witnessed ever encompassed the final acts of *Macbeth* until Olivier's second showing. I was spellbound sitting there watching – not him – no, it was *Richard III* all over again – the player disappeared, the part became the whole and the *whole* of Macbeth was revealed. I will quote here what he himself has written of this process:– "The work takes hold and takes over . . . with the first glimmer of invention or imagination I become lost in the magical wonder of being in its grip; one is barely conscious of the process by which one pours oneself."

Thus he showed us the searing ambition, the desperation of fear, the terrible remorse of his lines to Macduff:–

> But get thee back; my soul is too much charged
> With blood of thine already.

as no one had ever shown them to us before.

Great, toweringly great, performances. Wonderful to have lived in their time.

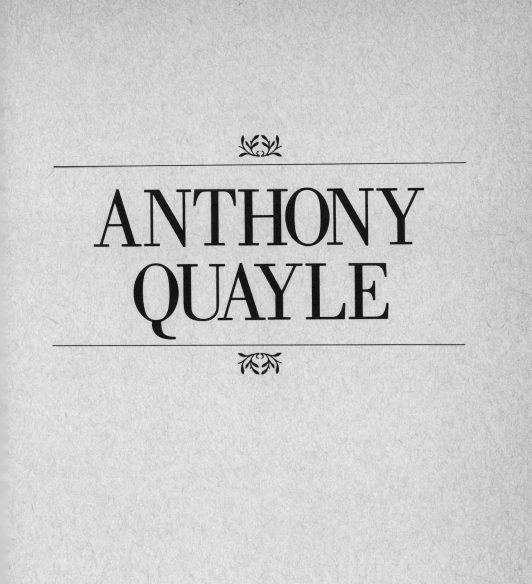

ANTHONY
QUAYLE

ANTHONY QUAYLE

It was during Anthony Quayle's directorship of the Stratford Memorial Theatre (now known as the Royal Shakespeare Company) between 1948 and 1956 that Olivier gave two of his greatest performances at Stratford. Later Quayle (b. 1913) toured Europe with Olivier in *Titus Andronicus*, in which he played Aaron. He was created CBE in 1952, and, in 1985, Knight. Recently he has played Oedipus in Sophocles's Theban plays, on television.

HALLEY'S COMET

He's a phenomenon: as fascinating, as spectacular as Halley's Comet. But there's a difference: Halley's Comet is only periodic, whereas Olivier has blazed steadily across the sky for the major part of my life. I was a scruffy student at the RADA and Larry was already a comet (or maybe a star) when I first met him. It was in the King's Road on the corner of Paultons Square: 1931, or thereabouts. I've still got a mental photo of him that day, hardly faded by time: a King's Road snapshot from a distinctly pre-punk era. He was the epitome of elegance: he wore a light-brown suit, a brown hat and co-respondent shoes; he had side-burns, trimmed dashingly on the slant, and he had two schnautzers on a lead. Not one: two. He was either on his way to, or coming back from, Hollywood; I don't remember which. I looked at him half in awe, half in jealousy, for the girl I was with was far more intrigued with him than she was with me. "My God!" I thought. "There's success for you. How can I ever achieve such lazy-lidded, devil-may-care, nonchalant assurance?" I must have been about nineteen and he must have been perhaps twenty-five; and those six years make a fearsome gap at that age. But it wasn't only the seniority in years that diminished me: it was the assurance of male beauty, of talent, of success.

A few years passed, and Larry was playing Henry V at the Old Vic: a production of Tyrone Guthrie's, and a big hit. I was asked to take over the Chorus from Marius Goring; Marius in his turn had taken over from Michael Redgrave; so I was number three.

The Chorus was obviously expendable. The night I opened, Larry, riding high on the spring-tide of success, came knocking on the door of my small dressing-room to wish me luck. He was utterly charming – and no man on earth can be more so. He wore a long, scarlet gown, leather-belted, and there was a simple crown on his cropped head; Harry Plantagenet himself dropping in to wish me well on his way to his rightful kingdom, the stage.

Larry has always been a king of the theatre. By that I don't mean to tag him with a simple label: "The Best" or "The Greatest". Those are newspaper epithets, resounding but hollow. There is no one "Best", for all are different. Every actor, every artist, makes his or her own individual contribution. In my lifetime the theatre has thrown up half a dozen "Greats", each of them running in different races, competing at different weights, indeed often aiming at different targets. In their own chosen field I have seen a few (a very few) surpass him. But Larry, with his talent, his magnetism, his single-mindedness, his wide-ranging energy assuredly walks away with the Decathlon.

I once heard Tyrone Guthrie say of him: "He is a nugget. It doesn't matter if he's not quite right in the part. It simply doesn't matter. He's a golden nugget."

That is exactly what he is, what he has always been: a nugget. And nine times out of ten he has been in the right part.

Look at his vast range of performances in the theatre: from Romeo to Titus Andronicus, from the Captain in *The Dance of Death* to Mr Puff in *The Critic*. On film the range is equally astonishing: from Heathcliff in *Wuthering Heights* and Max de Winter in *Rebecca* to the appalling dentist in *Marathon Man*. And he has triumphed not only in the monstrously difficult art of acting, which is a lifetime's work in itself, but also in theatre-management, in film-production. His three great Shakespearian films are a staggerng achievement. To produce, direct, and finally play the leading part in all three requires the energy and strength of Hercules.

Does that sound over-adulatory and therefore invalid? All right, then I will say that his Henry V was a performance I could not wholly admire. For my part, if I had had the misfortune to be a dysentery-riddled soldier at Agincourt, I could not have followed so narcissistic leader with much enthusiasm. But that is mere personal taste; it in no way detracts from the noble scale of the achievement.

There are at least three qualities that combine to explain the Olivier phenomenon. The first, of course, is sheer talent. Larry was born with that; but he has gone on and on, single-mindedly honing and sharpening his technical skills till there is virtually no act in the entire circus he cannot perform: perform, and excel in. His audacity makes you catch your breath. He can juggle; he can walk the slack-wire as well as the tight-rope; he can turn double somersaults in mid-air; he can train elephants; dammit, he can almost *be* an elephant.

The next quality is sheer animal magnetism. Larry has more of it than any actor I have known. That is what holds and dominates an audience. That is what makes a "star". And in Larry's case it has been magnetism backed up and controlled by a keen and ever-growing intelligence. *Charisma* is a word that has become fashionable, but I find it too affected and effete for the driving force that has emanated from Larry.

Third, I suppose, is ambition. No question but that Larry has had colossal ambition. Ours was the generation in the theatre that flowered before TV, before the "cult of personality". We were very disciplined in our theatre; we were brought up to subordinate ourselves, to be good members of the team. But I don't think that was ever for Larry. It's as though, almost from the start, he had said: "I am in no doubt as to what I am, and don't you be either. I am a highly unusual person and, what is more, I am a great, big, socking star. Just stand aside while I get on with it." And so he has. Juggling with all those bright balls, keeping four . . . six . . . eight of them in the air at once. Unique.

Is ambition a little unattractive? Is egotism something less than appealing? Perhaps. I only know I have never met a leader in any profession, in any walk of life, who was deficient in those two qualities. Larry has certainly had his full share of both. And thank God for it. Without them he would not be the man he is; he would not have done what he has done; he would not have climbed Mount Everest; and, having planted himself at the summit, he would not have been able for so long to keep his balance up there on top of the Himalayas.

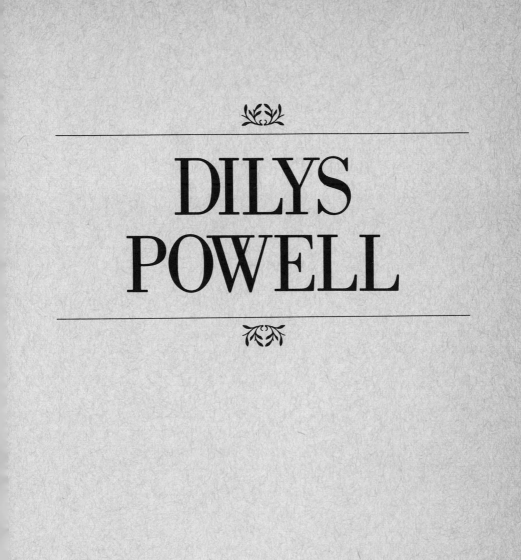

DILYS
POWELL

DILYS POWELL

The distinguished film critic Dilys Powell (CBE 1974) has been reviewing for fifty years. She is an Honorary Member of the ACTT, in 1984 received the BAFTA Award of Honour and in 1986 was made a Fellow of the British Film Institute. The author of five books, she lived in Athens in the 1930s, where her first husband, Humfry Payne, was director of the British School of Archæology.

THE EARLY FILMS

Athens is not a capital which provides an automatically welcoming audience, and it was in Athens that I first saw Paul Czinner's* film of *As You Like It*. It was 1936. The occasion was an echo of royalty – the accession to the British throne of George VI; and to mark it the British authorities had invited a high-society audience to the cinema. The film seemed, on the face of it, appropriate: Shakespeare, a romantic comedy, and a distinguished British cast; one felt a certain expectancy.

But this was half a century ago. The cinema had another decade to go before it could begin to manage Shakespeare – and fancy had got into the works. The Rosalind (it was Czinner's gifted wife, Elisabeth Bergner) scampered through the Forest of Arden with the air of a child playing bo-peep; the audience stilled its titters but not its well-bred disappointment. For the British it was an embarrassing occasion; and in the general dissatisfaction Laurence Olivier's performance as Orlando was scarcely noticed. Perhaps it was over-played; one finds that the Greeks themselves bring a powerful control to the performance of Shakespeare. All the same when years later the film was seen without the discomfort of a disapproving audience the quality of romantic passion in the Orlando was clear enough.

* Paul Czinner (1890–1972). German-born director who had previously directed (in 1926) a German version of *As You Like It*. He later made acclaimed film versions of Royal Ballet productions.

Even so, by 1936 Olivier was only beginning to get the feeling of the screen. He had been acting for the cinema for six years. In 1930 he was in a version of the stage play *Potiphar's Wife*. Directed by Maurice Elvey with a cast including Nora Swinburne, Norman McKinnel and Donald Calthrop, it presented the Old Testament figure in modern dress. A titled lady makes advances to her chauffeur; he rejects them and is falsely accused. Amusing to find a critic of 1931, throwing a bone to Olivier ("proves attractive as the chauffeur"), finding the theme "not in good taste".

The early thirties British cinema seemed to hold little for the young actor; he tried America. There were three American films. *Friends and Lovers*, directed by Victor Schertzinger, had Lily Damita married to Erich von Stroheim but indulging in affairs with Adolphe Menjou and Olivier. In *Westward Passage* the English actor was married, rather erratically, to Ann Harding; the director was Robert Milton. And *The Yellow Ticket*, adapted from a much earlier play about the Russian railway pass issued free to prostitutes, allowed Olivier to play a heroic figure; he rescued Elissa Landi from the unwelcome attentions of Boris Karloff and Lionel Barrymore; it was directed by Raoul Walsh.

Those of today's critics who have seen these early appearances in the American cinema find them not displeasing. We know, too, that Olivier was considered, though not chosen, for the role opposite Garbo in *Queen Christina*. All the same in 1932 he was back in England – and in some pretty ghastly cinema. Gertrude Lawrence also was trapped in *No Funny Business*, a piece about a pair sent to the Riviera by an agency to facilitate a divorce half-heartedly planned by a married couple; Jill Esmond, Olivier's wife at the time, was in the cast. And Gloria Swanson, in one of the many attempts to infuse life by importing Hollywood stars, appeared in *Perfect Understanding*, one of the marital movies which in this period dogged the actor.

But rescue was coming; Alexander Korda★ was on his way. The deliverance may not have seemed immediately obvious, but it was there; it was there in *Moscow Nights*. Not a remarkable film, though it had the famous Harry Baur as its unlikeable self-sacrificing star, though it had Korda as executive producer and the sensitive Anthony Asquith as director. But watching it now – especially

★ Alexander Korda (1893–1956). Hungarian-born director who became Britain's first film mogul. Created the Denham studio and London Films.

after looking at *No Funny Business* – one can see Olivier beginning to stretch himself, welcoming the chance of a romantic character. One mustn't pretend that the role of the Tsarist officer caught in gambling debts and charged with treason offers great scope. A display of anxiety as the defendant in a court-martial – well, it has its limits for the actor. But this actor was exceptionally handsome: that had its effect. There was the look of a romantic star.

A year later came *As You Like It* and the Orlando with its shade of exaggeration. By the mid-thirties Olivier had become a stage figure of international celebrity; perhaps – for stage technique clings – in the cinema he was still a stage actor. America, one is told, did not take to his performance in the British film *Fire Over England*. The Elizabethan age, Flora Robson as Elizabeth I, Raymond Massey as Philip of Spain, and the Armada threatening: Olivier's naval lieutenant is sent on a dangerous errand to Spain. The playing has the athletic drive of a popular star (Olivier was to be one of the most acrobatic of great players). But in the narrative the young man's father is captured by the Spaniards and burned at the stake. Confronted with the news, Olivier weeps; American audiences found that unmanly.

But the film, directed by the American William K. Howard, is interesting as showing the actor in slashabout action; an observer might have predicted a future in Hollywood adventure. Fortunately this was an actor in training, a man not to be diverted. The following year he was back in British non-adventure: *Twenty-One Days*, with Vivien Leigh in the cast, was a story of a killing concealed for the sake of a brother's career; it had a British director, Basil Dean. *The Divorce of Lady X* was better: an American director, Tim Whelan, Merle Oberon★ as the skittish wife trapped by fog who can't be dissuaded from sharing the divorce-lawyer's hotel bedroom, and a lively piece of comedy from Ralph Richardson as her husband. And Olivier, subjected to an ill-advised jest, for a moment shows the suppressed sullen temper which in later films was to strengthen his seductive force. Increasingly he was to be a sexual actor; it is a quality which goes much deeper than the romantic. Throughout the trifling comedy of *The Divorce of Lady X* he is pleasing, he is charming; sometimes one almost warms into laughter. It is not until the moment of affronted sexual vanity that he makes one care.

★ Merle Oberon (1917–79). Her first husband was Alexander Korda.

There was one more exercise: *Q Planes*, again directed by Tim Whelan – a light thriller with both Olivier and Ralph Richardson involved in a search for mysteriously disappearing British aircraft. Then Olivier took off – it was 1939 – for America. He was to play in a version of *Wuthering Heights* for Samuel Goldwyn.

A version: the narrative of the great novel was truncated, and the Cathy of Merle Oberon transported the Brontë landscape into suburbia. But an actor was there, an actor one had never seen on the screen before. The embers took fire; light blazed; with delighted astonishment one saw a new Olivier. The role of Heathcliff might have been made for him. We saw the despised boy and the romantic promise of youth; we saw the return after years of exile for the reward of fidelity – only to find the adored girl married, out of reach. Then he released the cold rage of cheated love. Olivier turned on the Edgar she had married a look of annihilating hate; it was a look unfamiliar to the cinema. It had scarcely faded from mind when the climax came: Cathy dying, Heathcliff kneeling at her bedside: Do not leave me in this dark abyss where I cannot find you! One will always remember that.

Something else one should remember. For the first time Olivier was directed by a major film-maker at the height of power. The experience transformed him. The qualities which had been greeted in the theatre were apparent now in the figure on the screen. And he acknowledged his debt. He acknowledged the part played in his development by the director of *Wuthering Heights*, William Wyler. It is difficult to find the conventional young player of the early British films of the thirties in the commanding actor he became in the forties. But the traces were there. Especially the quality of sexual force was there. And from *Wuthering Heights* onward it did not fail.

The Wyler film was a popular success. At the beginning of the war this country had a major stage actor who was also a major film star; he was to become a major creative director. I don't think general recognition immediately followed. Olivier continued playing in American cinema until 1941, when he came back to British films. I recall a meeting for journalists when he was present to talk about his forthcoming *Henry V*. He made a modest entry; it was interrupted by the arrival of David Niven (the Edgar of *Wuthering Heights*). Niven was an elegant performer who, perhaps because of his elegance, was often underrated, his capacity for pathos unrecognised; but he was a star, a film star. And attention at that journalistic gathering immediately shifted; Niven stole Olivier's thunder, somebody said. I don't think that would have happened a few years later; probably it would not have happened after the showing of *Henry V*. But on that occasion in 1944 it was noticeable: the star was more interesting than the actor.

Not that *Wuthering Heights* was the only movie to show the new Olivier qualities. Before he came back to Britain there had been other successes. *Rebecca* may not have been the best of Hitchcock, but it was admired. And it gave Olivier the opportunity for another display of chilly withdrawal: the seductive widower of Daphne du Maurier's story, having won his second wife, seems unable to sustain his devotion, incapable of sheltering her from the menace which hangs about the huge house; he is engulfed in inexplicable guilt and gloom. And there were two more successes in America. Once again in *Pride and Prejudice* the seductiveness of the withdrawn. Jane Austen's hero is too proud of his breeding to propose to the Elizabeth of Greer Garson, she is too much prejudiced against his loftiness to accept him. It is an English country society bustled up to please American audiences; family carriages race with one another to report a new social arrival. But the script had Aldous Huxley among its writers, and despite occasional absurdities it isn't a bad film. Anyway Olivier as Darcy preserves good taste; it is the performance of a gentleman. With *Lady Hamilton*, directed in America by Alexander Korda with Vivien Leigh in the title-part, Olivier's Nelson returns to romanticism, to heroism; the film is an attempt to draw a parallel between past history and the war being fought in 1941.

Then it was England again: British wartime themes, British directors, and two films which showed Olivier as a character actor. In *49th Parallel*, directed by Michael Powell, he was the French-Canadian trapper who encounters the Nazi submarine crew trying to make their way across Canada to a neutral refuge: in *The Demi-Paradise*, with Anthony Asquith directing, he was the Russian engineer posted to an English village and confronted by what is perhaps an excess of British eccentrics and British prejudice. Two humane, forthcoming figures to set against the cold heroes of a year or two earlier; they are remembered for their overwhelming charm. Olivier had reached a position in the cinema where he could choose. The next move was to the command of the Shakespeare versions.

Looking back on the progression from modest beginnings in

the cinema one sees that he was always the actor. Some film stars – some of the greatest – are not really actors or actresses. They exist by their presence; they are simply there. Olivier was never one of those; he has always been the actor. But the actor who has acquired the qualities of the cinema.

Look at the screen; he is its master.

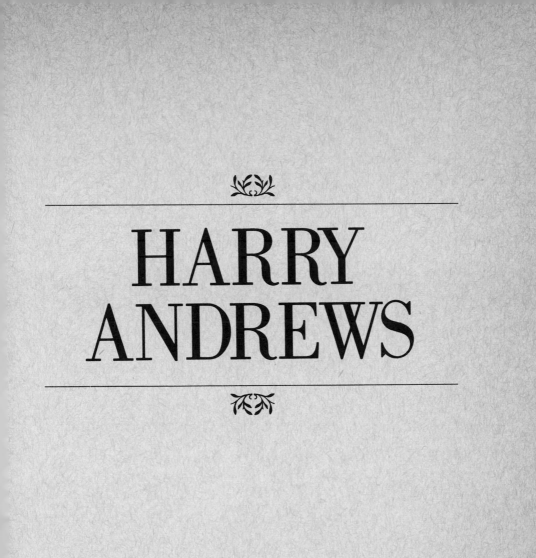

HARRY
ANDREWS

HARRY ANDREWS

Harry Andrews (b. 1911) was mentioned in dispatches in the second world war and has since put his military experience to good use in the notable soldiers he has played, although his successes have by no means been confined to the colours. He created the title role in Edward Bond's *Lear*, Ivan Kilner in Ronald Harwood's *A Family* and, in a recent revival of Osborne's *A Patriot For Me*, played The General. He was made a CBE in 1966.

COMPANIONS IN ARMS

In 1935 when Gielgud was preparing the production of *Romeo and Juliet* I was invited to be in it and I took over the part of Tybalt. Larry started by playing Romeo and Gielgud was playing Mercutio. Larry went for realism and gave a full-blooded passionate performance. "His blank verse is the blankest I've ever heard," said one critic; another, "He played Romeo as if he was riding a motorbike." I don't think the interpretation pleased Gielgud greatly, but there was no quarrel. There was certainly poetry in his movement and appearance. But when he played Mercutio we had the fight scene to do together. We were both physical people and Larry was a fine tennis player and very athletic. We were well rehearsed with two-handed swords and buckler and dagger, and we used to knock each other about quite a lot, slashing away as if we really meant it. Not a night passed without one of us causing the other some damage; years afterwards Larry often referred to this fight, saying he still bore the scars: it was a kind of rapport we both enjoyed.

In the war I was captain in the 15th Scottish Division. Towards the end of the fighting in Europe I was stationed about fifty miles away from Hamburg in an old Schloss. Richardson and Olivier brought the Old Vic Company over playing *Peer Gynt* and *Richard III*. They'd played in Paris, the Netherlands, and even given a performance to the garrison at Belsen and now were at the Stadtheatre, which hadn't been bombed while the rest of Hamburg was devastated. I took my boys over in three tonners to see the plays, and they'd never seen such acting, while most of them had never even been to a play. They were immensely impressed: I too. What was so wonderful was that Sybil Thorndike and Larry and Richardson were playing small parts in some of the plays and great parts in others. I said to the troops that if ever I got back to the theatre this was the kind of work I would like to be doing. Larry heard I was in front and asked to see me. "Let me know as soon as you get out of the army and there may be something for you in the company."

I never expected it would work. When I came out of the army, having been in uniform for six years, I took my courage in both hands and went to see him. Round at the stage door, I met his dresser, who recognised me and called him away from all his grand friends and he came over and said, "Look, Harry, give me your telephone number and address and I'll ring you." Soon afterwards he did, and fixed me up with the parts that George Curzon had been playing. I had three first nights to face in a row: in *Oedipus* and Part One and Two of *Henry IV*. After all those years I found going on stage terrifying. Sybil Thorndike, I remember, was wonderful to me as an actor coming back into the business after such a long break. "Learn a verse of the bible every night and you'll never have a worry," she told me. I never did do that and I *did* worry! Larry, too, went out of his way to help me during that difficult period.

But he had a streak of ruthlessness. This manifested itself in the way he could be professionally jealous of people, even of his old chum Ralph Richardson. When they were playing *Henry IV*, *Part One* as Hotspur and Falstaff, usually the applause at the end when they were taking their solo bows, rose to a peak when Larry came on and died a little bit when Ralph took his. One night, however, I was holding the curtain for him to go on and receive his applause and Ralphy came on just after him and it rose well above his and he said, "Hell, the bastard, why the hell has he done that to me?" And he meant it.

His judgement wasn't always spot on. But he knew where he wanted to go. Single-mindedness is the equipment of all great achievement. An incident in which I was involved illustrates this. In 1958, I think it was, I had just been asked to play Coriolanus in the following 1959 gala season at Stratford by Glen Byam Shaw, when Larry rang me and asked me down to Notley for the weekend. I said I'd be delighted, and when I was there, on Sunday over drinks, he asked me what plans I had. I told him about Byam Shaw's offer. "Marvellous, you must do it." "But," I said, "I wasn't sure if I'd be right for it: hadn't Glen already asked him," I said. Larry answered, "Well as a matter of fact he asked me about six months ago but I turned it down. It might now, I think, be a good idea." "In that case, Larry," I told him, "you must do it." Throughout, Larry behaved very tactfully towards me, so did Glen, who insisted I do it but finally I rang Peter Hall, asking him, "Surely it would be very exciting for you as director to have Larry in the part?" "If you put it like that the answer is yes," he replied. In short, I bowed out, and stayed with another good part, that of Menenius, in the production. There was no bad feeling. And it was a tremendous success all round.

The projected film of *Macbeth* had a less fortunate outcome. Alan Dent and Vivien and he had got together and concocted this wonderful screen version of the play. There was a lot of preparatory work, including trips to Scotland. I was to play Macduff, and looking forward to it enormously: to being out in the open, to Lady Macbeth coming out of the castle on a horse, to the witches on the moor: the whole thing was richly and imaginatively thought out. Then, very near the time, the backers opted out and the whole thing was cancelled. He was forced to go into *The Devil's Disciple* with Kirk Douglas and Burt Lancaster. He told the directors, "I want Harry Andrews in it, because he was to play Macduff." So I played Major Swindon, a boring character, but quite funny I suppose. During shooting Larry was upset, I think, about not being allowed to do Macbeth. It's the only time I've seen him lacking slightly in confidence, but as usual he walked away with the film playing General Burgoyne.

I went to Notley many times. Larry adored playing the local squire in this ancient and baronial home, pruning the hedges and preparing the ground for sowing. Vivien was wonderful in the garden: there were servants and dinners and the wine was very good – it was almost out of some old film. Sometimes – and she wasn't all that well – Vivien would get up at five and start doing the weeding, dead heading and planting, and you'd see her from your bedroom window. You'd call down, "Oh darling, when are you going to have breakfast?" Larry, of course, would be sleeping. It couldn't last for ever. One was very privileged to go there and enjoy all the glamour and dressing up for dinner. I remember him once saying to me as we were driving to Stratford together to do

Coriolanus, "Well, now my baronial period is just about over, I'm not sure what comes next."

When the time came to sell the place I happened to be there at a weekend when some Americans came to look at it. It was a sad occasion. Things are different now. He likes to wear braces and enjoys being the "common" man!

MICHAEL BILLINGTON

MICHAEL BILLINGTON

Born in 1939, Michael Billington has been drama critic of the *Guardian* since 1971. He has written numerous books, including *The Modern Actor, How Tickled I am, The Guinness Book of Theatrical Facts and Feats,* and *Alan Ayckbourn.* He first saw Olivier act in the mid-1950s, and has followed his work closely for thirty years.

LASCIVIOUSLY PLEASING

"I may be rather feminine but I'm not effeminate." This remark, revealing and unprompted, was made to me by Laurence Olivier over pre-lunch drinks one day at Broadcasting House in 1982. He had come in to record a half-hour tribute to Ralph Richardson for his eightieth birthday. I had never spent any time in the great man's company before and was very struck by his slightly raffish coyness. At one point we were chatting about Olivier's rare excursions into radio and he revealed that he had once played Pandulph in a BBC production of *King John* at Savoy Hill. I remarked that it was a pity that the play was so rarely done adding – for want of anything better to say – that last time out it had been massively adapted by John Barton.★ "Ah," said Olivier with what I can only call a twinkle, "he's a saucebox, that one." I had never previously thought of John Barton in quite those terms.

I repeat this anecdote only because it provides a clue to part of Olivier's titanic greatness as an actor: his sexual contradictoriness. He can be masculine and feminine but never neuter. When I was an Oxford undergraduate Peter Hall, then directing Olivier in *Coriolanus* at Stratford, came down to give a talk to OUDS. Eager for insight and gossip, we asked him what he thought Olivier's most distinctive quality was: "his sexiness" was Hall's instant

★ John Barton (b. 1928). A close associate of Peter Hall at Stratford. His Shakespearian adaptations, *The Hollow Crown* and *The Wars of the Roses*, are celebrated.

71

reply. When I saw the performance later, I got his point: Olivier leapt lightly over the sexual frontiers and suggested that inside the ruggedly arrogant Roman general lurked an element of girlish shyness. Good actors exist securely inside a mono-sexual world. Great performers – an Olivier, a Garbo, a Dietrich, a Chaplin – are often flecked by sexual ambiguity. They embrace opposites and in that way exert a magnetic hold over us: as Henry James pointed out, one test of a great player is that you instantly start to speculate about his or her private personality.

I am not arguing that this is the major part of Olivier's appeal but it is one of the cards in an unusually rich hand. Amongst the others I would place a formidable interpretative intelligence that intuitively searches for new meanings in the great classic roles; an incisive voice that has the directional force and cutting edge of a laser; eyes that can communicate powerful emotion over a large distance; a physical daring that enables him not merely to undertake death-defying leaps but to alter his physical equipment to suit the demands of the role (witness the muscularity of his Othello); a mimetic relish that may spring, if we are to believe *Confessions of an Actor*, from self-doubt and even self-disgust; a boundless energy that has meant, over the years, that each new Olivier performance was as much a creative event as, say, a new novel by Graham Greene or a new film from Orson Welles. Of younger actors, only McKellen and Sher give me that sense that each new role is a special occasion, yet another mountain to be climbed.

But my theme is Olivier's stage sexuality and his ability to embrace sexual opposites. I became aware of it the first time I saw Olivier on stage which was at Stratford in 1955 in a rather sedate, refined production of *Twelfth Night* by Gielgud. Olivier's Malvolio was not much acclaimed or even noticed (the production opened during a newspaper-strike) but it was a highly original creation: beak-nosed, crinkly-haired, palpably Jewish, a tormented social and racial outsider. But what I remember is Olivier's walk which was a dainty, fairy-footed progress across the stage with the skittish, faintly epicene lightness of a great comic like Bob Hope or Jack Benny. Olivier's Malvolio – a working-class Jewish boy who'd made good in Illyria – was also racked by difficulties of pronunciation. When he came to the phrase in Olivia's assumed letter "Cast thy humble slough" he agonised over whether the noun should sound like the name of the Berkshire town or whether it should be "sluff". It was camp. It was also funny. And it told

72

us a lot about Malvolio's terrifying insecurity. A footnote: I recall attending the last night of the season when everyone expected one of Olivier's famous curtain speeches thanking everyone down to the stage-doorman. As the applause died, Olivier advanced timorously to the footlights and cried, in a voice of shrill, Arthur Marshall–schoolmistress horror, "But I haven't prepared one!" Of course, he had.

A year later I spent a day in the Regal Cinema, Leamington Spa sitting twice through Olivier's film of *Richard III*. This performance, as much as any, reveals Olivier's ability to reconcile seemingly opposite qualities: evil and charm, calculation and impulse, directness and irony. But a thread running consistently through the performance is Olivier's sly, feminine roguishness. Tynan noted in the stage performance "the deep concerns as of a bustling spinster with which Olivier grips his brother George and says with sardonic effeminate intentness 'We are not safe, Clarence, we are not safe', while even as he speaks the plot is laid which will kill the man." Look at the film and you notice the saucy roll of the eyes with which Olivier, in the opening soliloquy, directs our attention to "the lascivious pleasing of a lute", the deeply ambiguous raising of a black-gloved hand to indicate the heavenward progress of Lady Anne's husband, the play of the tongue against the teeth as he confides "I'll have her . . . but I will not keep her long." Olivier's Richard has the twinkling malevolence of a maiden-aunt with psychopathic tendencies. But the brilliance of this bustling femininity is that it offsets a profound, murderous masculinity. Neil Simon in *The Goodbye Girl* lampoons the idea of a flamboyantly gay, Off-Broadway Richard III. Olivier's Richard is not that but a uniquely sinister amalgam of male power-hunger and female seductiveness.

This ironic use of mock-femininity is something one associates more with comics than with straight actors. Jack Benny, dapper and blazered, would underscore a line like "I'm not saying I'm heavily insured but when I go, *they* go," with the flap of a limp wrist. Bob Hope, at the faintest whiff of danger, would rattle his teeth like dice in a box and leap into the nearest woman's arms. Our own magnificent Frankie Howerd is Sairey Gamp in gaberdine clothing: a tumultuous gossip who looks nervously over his shoulder before confiding with sibilant intensity, as he did at one Awards dinner, that he has found the perfect partner for Edward Heath – "*Dorothy* Squires".

John Osborne exploited both the vein of studied camp in front-cloth comics and the strain of sexual ambivalence in Olivier's stage-persona in creating Archie Rice in *The Entertainer*. This, along with the Stratford Macbeth and Captain Edgar in *The Dance of Death*, was one of Olivier's greatest hours. It was a performance filled with pain, agony, self-disgust and soaring eloquence when Olivier's voice hit a rising arc of feeling as he described the "beautiful fuss" he once heard made by a black gospel-singer in a bar. But in the front-cloth scenes Olivier's Archie with his gap-teeth, thickly-painted eyebrows, rouged cheeks, centre-parting and wisps of grey hair was the very essence of music-hall camp. I have before me, as I write, a wonderful picture from the cover of *Encore* magazine in the summer of 1957 with Olivier's Archie looking leeringly skywards while, from inside the frame of his raised titfer, his teak-skinned, laurel-bound Titus Andronicus gazes stonily on. It is a graphic double-image of Olivier: the gnarled soldier and the ambisextrous comic. "You think I'm like that, don't you? You think I am. Well I'm not. But *he* is." Olivier turned Archie's patter into lewd sexual riddle-me-ree.

But my point is that Olivier does not parcel his performances up into those with a strong masculine or feminine bias: he constantly allows the two elements to interact. His Stratford Coriolanus in 1959 left behind its own dark, sombre imprint: I can hear him even now crying "I banish *you*" as he turned his back on the treacherous populace. But when Olivier was forced to kiss his wife publicly in his garlanded return from battle he shifted uneasily from foot to foot and rolled his eyes in embarrassment like a nervous Prom Queen. And in the famous admonition scene, when Volumnia urges Coriolanus to behave with politic moderation in his confrontation with the people, Olivier played with the word "mildly" in a manner that was comic and ironic and indicative of a teasing rebellion against a lifetime of mother-domination. Olivier's Coriolanus was consummately virile but specked with tell-tale hints of some banked-down alternative quality.

I have no wish to overstate the case or to suggest that Olivier's stage-persona is one of candid bisexuality: I merely suggest that he frequently deploys qualities of silkiness, irony, mischief, vulnerability, intensity that, in our society, are more often thought of as feminine than masculine. Acting is perhaps one way of overcoming the sexual stereotyping of conventional society. I talked some time ago to Vanessa Redgrave who had recently played a trans-sexual doctor and tennis-player in an American TV film, *Second Serve*. She recalled how, as a six-foot tall teenager in the 1950s, she had been made to feel unwomanly and, when dancing with someone, was often obliged to take the male role. But playing the trans-sexual Renee Richards had heightened her awareness of "the way male and female are incredibly interwoven in all of us" and, I suspect, had an unacknowledged influence on her Haymarket Cleopatra. Shortly after this I interviewed Bob Hoskins about *Mona Lisa* and he revealed that he had learned most about acting from women because they can express a private moment or a hidden thought without saying a word. "In acting," said Mr Hoskins, "you've got to use the feminine side of you. I don't mean the limp wrist but what are still considered the feminine qualities: vulnerability, affection, tenderness. I think a really dignified person is someone who allows all that to show and is not afraid to be themselves."

What younger actors articulate, Olivier has always done instinctively: that is to display *all* aspects of the human personality without shame, modesty or fear. Even at his butchest Olivier slips in hints of a dandified vanity: one remembers that astonishing first entrance in *Othello* with a red rose held gently between thumb and forefinger and with the hips rotating slightly in a manner half way between Dorothy Dandridge and Gary Sobers. Conversely, Olivier's fops leave you in no doubt as to their ultimate masculinity: His Captain Brazen in the 1963 *Recruiting Officer* made a high-speed entrance in a chestnut wig and planted a resounding kiss on the cheeks of a male friend but the well-pitched military camp concealed a heterosexual resolve. Likewise his Tattle in the 1965 *Love For Love* was a gossiping fribble who at one point dandy-minced it across the tops of stone-walls but whose designs on Miss Prue were aimed squarely below the belt. It is a modern fallacy that fops are homosexual. Olivier's two Restoration performances reminded us that in the seventeenth-century finery of apparel and frivolity of manner were compatible with balls. The paradox of all this is that Olivier is the ultimate Protean actor.

PETER USTINOV

PETER USTINOV

Born in London in 1921, Peter Ustinov served during the war in the Royal Sussex Regiment and the RAOC, where he began developing his rich and diverse talents, later winning himself a worldwide reputation as playwright, actor, director and designer. A celebrated wit and autobiographer too, he was awarded the Order of the Smile for dedication to the idea of international assistance to children (Warsaw, 1974). Rector of Dundee University for six years, he received the CBE in 1975.

INTEGRITY
AN EXPENSIVE
BUSINESS

A group of students had seen the dress rehearsal of *Macbeth* because it was directed by Michel Saint-Denis, who was our guru. Afterwards we went to the only kind of place which a student could go to which was open that late, a restaurant called Old Vienna, part of the Lyons Corner House. There in the corner, in a kind of tryst, sat Larry Olivier and Vivien Leigh. They were all the rage at the time and we munched our sandwiches in awe. The place was empty except for all of us at one end, and the two of them at the other.

He was a very energetic actor. Macbeth wasn't one of his happiest performances, especially as there have been so many happier ones, and Michel Saint-Denis had not as much to contribute to *Macbeth* as he might have done to something more reticent. I always thought of him as a director who admired imagination, but didn't possess that much himself. He never quite liberated himself from the influence of Jacques Copeau, his uncle.

When Olivier was gaining his spurs, *Romeo and Juliet* was regarded quite wrongly as a kind of conflict between him and Gielgud. I hate those competitions. It was like Kemble and Kean. I knew whom Larry was modelling himself on because very much later I got a telephone call from Jock Dent, a great friend of the Oliviers, at the time critic of the *News Chronicle*. He rang to ask me to collaborate on a screen play. He wasn't yet able to tell me the name or nature of the screen play, but I said, "It's going to be *Edmund Kean*." After a long pause on the line he said, "Well, our provisional title is *The Life and Death of Edmund Kean.*" I hadn't foreseen the all-embracing nature of the work, but I was sure Larry was fascinated by Kean.

Kean, of course, had his enemies as well, and Kemble had his fanatics although probably Kemble was a rather boring actor, very distinguished and boring, which was not at all like John Gielgud, except that John has the same kind of magnificence and reticence. When I was stationed in Salisbury during the war as a private soldier, saving my pocket money up for a bar of Fry's Chocolate Cream and the odd book – Salisbury is a wonderful town with bookshops which remaindered all sorts of works at sixpence – I picked up a work called *Theatrical Inquisitor*, wherein a contemporary enemy of Kean wrote, "Either Mr Kean is energetic or he is nothing!"

This is not a criticism of Larry Olivier, except that in order to have so many qualities one must have defects as well. His Richard III was absolutely staggering, but I didn't really care for his Hamlet because it was supposed to be a man who couldn't make up his mind – or advertised as such – and one of Larry's shortcomings is that he can't play anybody who can't make up his mind, because he's made up his about so many things on his way to the character.

I never find him quite as good in ordinary parts when he's pretending to be estate agents or things like that. This is something he shares with Richard Burton, whom I once saw rehearsing the remake of *Brief Encounter*, which was a mistake anyway. Burton walked up to a kiosk and he said, "Can I have a cup of tea, please." One thought, what does that mean, is it some sort of password belonging to a secret organisation? The last thing that entered one's mind was that he wanted a cup of tea. Larry is similar. His diction is so precise that he simply can't resist giving everything a certain amount of importance.

His greatest assets are extraordinary stamina, and extraordinary power – a sort of controlled recklessness. I say controlled advisedly, because he's a political animal as well, and therefore one likes him enormously at moments when he is disarming, and looks at him with slight misgiving when he is trying to organise something. I'm judging him from a neutral point of view, as one who was engaged in the same business in a rather different sense. When the Old Vic was starting I was still very much in view as a dramatist, and they wanted me to write a play specially for them. I went to see them, and John Burrell, who was then in charge, said, "Just write anything you think of." Larry was a bit more, but not terribly, specific; Ralph Richardson said, "Give us something we can sing and dance and make merry!" The whole commission seemed to me slightly sinister.

His predilection for putting on false noses very often resembling the nose he has anyway, is a method of hiding and sheltering him. An outward manifestation of a certain timidity apart from his buoyancy. He is not nearly as much at ease being himself as he is being someone else; in that sense he's a character actor by nature. When he's forced to make maiden speeches in the House of Lords, or speeches acknowledging victories in Oscar competitions, they are always so convoluted it looks rather like Dr Bowdler at work on Shakespeare. I was rather disappointed with his book, written in the same style; I wished he'd put on a false nose and be himself again.

Charles Laughton, of course, without the temptation of being a leading man because nature wasn't generous to him with good looks, was completely a character actor. I always had a vision of them at the wheel of racing cars, Olivier always in the lead, but everytime he looked in his driving mirror there was Charles Laughton's face, mouthing, "I can overtake you whenever I choose," which was not quite true, but was all the same a menace. And their differences were very, very clear-cut. Larry tried to give Laughton some hints of where to stand on the Stratford stage when he was going to play King Lear. Larry, with his sense of being liked and being helpful, did this absolutely altruistically. Laughton, with his oversensitivity, convinced that everybody was trying to trip him up, was sure it was out of sheer bitchiness. He thought the places to stand were completely different, and that he would not be audible from those indicated by Larry. That was a typical conflict.

And then, of course, they rubbed each other the wrong way in other senses. They had a scene in the Roman senate in *Spartacus* which started off with Laughton among the other senators asking pertinent questions about ancient Rome in a slightly Yorkshire accent to Laurence Olivier, who was standing there as the new victor of some sort of political situation. Laughton played the scene frightfully well, rather sidelong, not really looking at Larry. Then they did the reverse shots on Larry addressing him, and eventually Larry couldn't concentrate and blew his lines once or twice and asked to do it without Laughton there.

Laughton's exit from the senate was much more real than anything in the film. A sort of outsize mannequin at Swan and Edgar's dowagers' department, walking out with tremendous dignity and suffering. And then Larry did it perfectly to nothing. I was the catalyst in the middle of all this; both confided in me believing that I was on their side and not neutral.

There was something about them that was fundamentally and basically antagonistic, although both of them would probably have denied it. Larry always had an acute sense of hierarchy and how to behave, and what his ambitions should be, while Laughton was the man who'd made his concession, who said often, "acting is whoring", and said it with the satisfaction of a highly successful whore. At the same time, while Larry was struggling with laundry bills, trying to make ends meet in Hollywood on the amount of money he was allowed by the British exchange control, there was Laughton in his own house, floating in his own pool, surrounded by Renoirs and pre-Columbian artefacts. He had made his compromise, but had all the things he wanted. He had a very cultivated mind and thought of acting as a means to an end. He started reading the Bible altruistically and then became commercially successful at it. He lived a civilised life according to his own lights and I don't think he gave a damn whether he had a knighthood or not.

In *Spartacus* Larry was determined to do everything authentically and knew that the Romans didn't have stirrups. He rode his horse without a saddle. Kubrick begged him not to because he had a very sensitive lens on the camera and even a quarter inch variation would hurt the shot. Larry still insisted. The horse moved always during the line and always had to be cut. After take sixteen or seventeen Larry agreed to sit on top of a ladder. Moments later he fell off, and hurt himself. It was not the kind of ladder he was destined to stay at the top of.

He has an absolutely disarming and very friendly quality and I hope I was able to reciprocate this. When he was at the beginning of his relationship with Joan Plowright,* and the press was haring after him all the time, he came to Rome for some reason and we put him up and fetched him from the airport. I got permission

---

* Joan Plowright (b. 1929) first appeared with Olivier in John Osborne's *The Entertainer* in 1957. They married in 1961.

from the customs officials to drive my car on to the tarmac and rescue him from the press. We took him out as freight.

Long before I visited Notley once. He and Vivien were always surrounded by a kind of *quadrilla*. They called each other "Boy" and I always felt slightly left out of these cordial goings-on because I'm not a joiner by nature. If I'm asked to join a march for this or that reason, or sign a document protesting against some sort of human behaviour, I can't do it. Vivien sat like a cat on the sofa and said very little and seemed to dominate him by not saying anything. Everytime he looked at her he would start becoming more buoyant and more aggressive.

When I retired for the night I found there was a slight pressure on my feet the whole time, as though somebody had left a copy of *Life Magazine* on the bed, just annoying enough to make me think, "What the hell is this, there's a weight on my toes." Eventually it became an obsession so I got up and undid the bed. The maid had done the sheets the wrong way round and there was an enormous monogram with L.O. and V.L. intertwined, which should have been at the top and was down at the feet. Once I knew what it was I could put up with it.

When we were both up for the same Emmy award in America he cabled the American television authorities to say that if he won he would like me to accept it for him. I thought to myself, this is a bit thick, but didn't say anything. By some miracle I won it, and said, "I regret I haven't prepared a speech. I've only prepared a speech for Laurence Olivier – had he won – and I'd better give you that."

He has a wonderful social sense and an admirable sense of humour about himself. I love the story which I heard about him being asked by some foreign people what O.M. meant, and he barked, "Old Man!"

SHERIDAN MORLEY

SHERIDAN MORLEY

One of the best television interviews of Olivier was done by Sheridan Morley (b. 1941) for BBC's *Late Night Line-up*. He is the drama critic and arts editor of *Punch*, and has written many books on the theatre, including biographies of Noël Coward, Gladys Cooper and David Niven (*The Other Side of the Moon*).

OLIVIER
AND HIS
CRITICS

"There is, you see, a gulf fixed between good and great performances," wrote Kenneth Tynan* in 1953, "but a bridge spans it over
which you may stroll if your visa is in order . . . Olivier pole-vaults
over in a single animal leap; Gielgud, seizing a parasol, crosses by
tightrope; Redgrave, ignoring this, always chooses the hard way.
He dives into the torrent and tries to swim across, usually sinking
within sight of the shore."

What Richardson did about the torrent, Tynan never got around
to telling us; perhaps the wily stage magician merely walked across
the water. But of those four great classical actor-knights of his
own generation, Olivier until quite late in his stage career was
the one who usually divided critics most sharply. Those who
responded with enthusiasm to the "great animal leap" were those
reviewers like Tynan, and before him James Agate, who were
forever in search of the high-definition performance rather than
scholastic safety on stage, those in fact who went to the theatre
hoping to sniff the scent of danger that so often surrounded
Olivier's work.

"There was a bizarre impression of one man lynching a crowd,"
wrote Laurence Kitchen of his "common cry of curs" speech in
Coriolanus, while William Wyler (who directed him in *Wuthering
Heights* and *Carrie* and who in 1944 Olivier wanted as the director

---

* Kenneth Tynan (1927–80) was at this point beginning to make his reputation
as a drama critic, joining the *Observer* the following year.

of *Henry V* before being told by Wyler to do it himself) added, "Larry is like a panther: just when you think you know where he is and that you've got him cornered, he springs out at you from some totally different direction." But British theatre critics as a breed did not always take kindly to the springs of a panther, and Olivier made his own feelings about his reviewers clear enough in *On Acting*:

> I suppose critics are a grim necessity. There are good ones and bad ones, and ones who simply masquerade as critics but are mere purveyors of columns of gossip, tittle-tattle signifying nothing. Poor creatures who are pushed by their pens and not by their intellects. The good ones are essayists and of immense value to our work. They help, sometimes hinder, but most understand the problems and pitfalls of our profession. Without them some of the great performances of the past would have gone by unrecorded . . . I know that if we are foolish enough to parade ourselves between spotlight and reality, we must be prepared to receive the attention of the pen . . . I have been battered and bruised, praised and lauded. I have laughed and cried, fumed and snorted; I have been beyond the moon and into the depths of despair. But in the end, it has been myself I've had to turn to, believe in and listen to.

Not that he was always so mellow in his attitude to critics: forty years earlier, directing Vivien Leigh in the London première of Thornton Wilder's *The Skin of Our Teeth*, Olivier noticed James Agate slipping back into his seat ten minutes after an interval had ended. Furious that he should have missed an important scene, Olivier went over to Agate and struck him sharply across the shoulder while whispering "You're late, blast you." The *Sunday Times* review was, all things considered, remarkably favourable and it could well be argued that when he was forming his National Theatre team in 1963 Olivier achieved his final revenge on critics by the simple device of granting Tynan his request to become the National's literary manager, thereby efficiently silencing the foremost reviewer of his generation. By thus castrating "the little bastard" as Olivier at one point in his memoirs refers to Tynan, he also ensured a relatively gentle ride for the opening of the new management at the Old Vic.

But Olivier's earliest reviewers were two legendary theatrical *grandes dames*: Ellen Terry, seeing him at the age of ten as Brutus in a schoolboy *Julius Caesar* at All Saints' in London noted "the boy is already an actor" while a few years later, when he played Katherina in a schoolboy *Taming of the Shrew* at Stratford, his first appearance in a real theatre, the audience included Sybil Thorndike since her father and his were churchmen with neighbouring parishes. She too recognised "a born actor" though his first public notice was rather less welcome: of *A Midsummer Night's Dream* at St Edward's in Oxford where he was now a pupil, the local paper reported "the boy who played Puck, although he had a potent stage presence, emoted with frantic and altogether unnecessary effect, as though playing a joke on his fellow cast members instead of the audience." It was only in 1930, during the London run of *Private Lives*, that Noël Coward finally convinced Olivier the idea of comedy was for the audience to laugh at the actors, not for the actors to giggle at one another.

By the time he reached the Central School in 1924, critical opinion was already divided about him: Henry Oscar, one of his tutors and himself a character actor of considerable skill, reckoned that he would never overcome a lack of grace and untidy appearance, though Athene Seyler, seeing him as Shylock in an end-of-term *Merchant of Venice* which also featured the young Peggy Ashcroft, thought well of an actor who "did not hand you his whole performance on a plate but left you to discover him".

His first professional notice came in 1925 when he was cast in a small role for a curtain-raiser that toured with *The Ghost Train*: on his first entrance he managed to trip over a door frame and, noted the local paper, "Mr Laurence Olivier made a good deal of a rather minor part." One-line reviews were the most he could hope for at this early stage in his career but one of these ("Mr Olivier had little to do, but he *acted*" from St John Ervine in the *Observer*) helped to establish him in Barry Jackson's Birmingham Rep in 1926 and two years later, when Jackson brought him to the Royal Court, it was Ervine who wrote the first really thoughtful notice about Olivier:

> He varies in his performance but he is excellent on the whole and has the makings of a very good actor in him. His faults are those of inexperience rather than ineffectiveness. The good performance he gave in *Macbeth* (as Malcolm) added to the good

performance he gives in *Harold* make me believe that when romantic and poetic drama return to their proper place in the theatre, Mr Olivier will be ready to occupy the position of a distinguished romantic actor.

Agate for the *Sunday Times* was not so easily or instantly won over: "Mr Olivier's Bothwell," he wrote of the 1934 *Queen of Scots* "is a little too light, especially in the voice which has the tennis club 'Will you serve first partner or shall I?' ring about it." By this time Olivier had also made some early appearances on film, though *Picturegoer* dismissed him in the 1931 *Friends and Lovers* as "altogether too precious" and Greta Garbo had dismissed him altogether from the set of *Queen Christina* in favour of John Gilbert. Opposite Gertrude Lawrence in the 1933 *No Funny Business*, the *Monthly Film Bulletin* found "Mr Olivier looking somewhat unhappy as the conventional juvenile lead" and students of his early movie roles could be forgiven for thinking they were watching a man who had just missed second prize in a Ronald Colman lookalike contest.

On stage, while he attracted generally good reviews for his appearances in modern dress (*Private Lives*, 1930; *Rats of Norway*, 1933) there was a certain critical uneasiness about his verse-speaking in Shakespeare. Where Gielgud would go for the music of a line, Olivier went for the emotion: "By leading up to the emphatic isolation of a single word," recalled Harold Hobson, "he repeatedly swept away the audience in a flood of feeling, only to find himself the next morning critically reviled for not having treated poetry as if it were a kind of ever-flowing brook or ceaselessly-ticking metronome." When, therefore, Olivier and Gielgud alternated Romeo and Mercutio to the Juliet of Peggy Ashcroft in 1935, battle lines were sharply drawn: the *Evening Standard* noted "Mr Olivier can play many parts but Romeo is not one of them: his voice has neither the tone nor the compass and his verse is the blankest I ever heard. When Miss Ashcroft asked him 'Wherefore art thou Romeo?', I was inclined to echo her question"; while for the *Sunday Times* Agate complained "Mr Olivier's Romeo suffered enormously from the fact that the spoken poetry of the part eluded him. In his delivery he brought off a twofold inexpertness which approached virtuosity – that of gabbling all the words in a line and uttering each line as a staccato whole cut off from its fellows."

For the *Observer* however, St John Ervine reckoned "I have seen few sights so moving as the spectacle of Mr Olivier's Romeo, stunned with Juliet's beauty, fumbling for words with which to say his love . . . I am not bold enough to say what Shakespeare would or would not have liked, but I think his eyes would have shone had he seen this Romeo young and ardent and full of clumsy grace."

From the Birmingham Rep seasons of the late 1920s there and in London, where a young Ralph Richardson also came to the attention of early talent scouts, Olivier seemed to have then abandoned the classics for such modern costume pieces as *Beau Geste* and *Queen of Scots*, or else for drawing-room dramas like *Biography* and *The Green Bay Tree* and the Barrymore parody *Theatre Royal*. With his return to Shakespeare in the middle Thirties came the first thoughtful assessments of his qualities as an actor and how they distinguished him from his immediate contemporaries:

"When Mr Gielgud played Mercutio he gave us the cascade but failed at the bluff," thought Charles Morgan for *The Times*. "There is plenty of honest rock about Mr Olivier's Mercutio, though he turns on the poetry in the way that athletic young fellows turn on the morning bath."

A year later, Olivier was leading the Old Vic company as Hamlet and Henry V and Toby Belch and then into the 1937 season as Macbeth and Coriolanus and Iago to Richardson's Othello: given that line-up of roles, there was now no way that any critic could fail to take account of his place at the forefront of the classical theatre, even though some were still doubtful about his right to be there. Alan Dent for the *Manchester Guardian* found the Hamlet "in general bearing so bloody, bold and resolute that it is inconceivable that he could allow any philosophic qualm or query to stand between him and immediate regicide". The Henry V Dent found "an unending series of iambics mounting semitone by semitone and delivered in a quite arbitrary sequence of crescendos and diminuendos. The end result reminded one irresistibly of the monotonous rise and fall of telegraph wires along a railway track". The Iago for Dent was "altogether too light and unsubtle, merely a roguish skylarker", though he did approve of the Macbeth and the Coriolanus and was, even with these reservations, already among Olivier's more enthusiastic supporters.

In general however it was from film rather than theatre critics that Olivier was now receiving the accolades, regardless of his own distrust and early dislike of the new medium: "Laurence

Olivier seems to me to be one of the most brilliant actors in the world," wrote Campbell Dixon of his first Shakespearian film *As You Like It*, "and his triumph as Orlando is all the more striking for its contrast to his glamorous Romeo and his fiery Mercutio in John Gielgud's recent stage production."

The Vic seasons were followed by four major movie appearances (*Fire Over England*, *Wuthering Heights*, *Rebecca* and *Pride and Prejudice*) which again divided critics on both sides of the Atlantic. His Heathcliff, thought Frank Nugent, "is one of those once in a lifetime things, a case of a player physically and emotionally ordained for a role . . . Olivier is Heathcliff, heaven-sent to Brontë and Goldwyn"; while for Graham Greene in the *New Statesman* "his nervous, breaking voice belongs to balconies and Verona and romantic love". Agate for the *Tatler* was more enthusiastic:

> Not being Irving, Chaliapin and Conrad Veidt all rolled into one, Mr Olivier does not give a superhuman performance. But the performance he does give is extremely good and suggests what I take to be very important, that somewhere in Heathcliff's dark soul there is a spot of something which might in another world or dimension grow to compunction. Or shall I put it that in this film Mr Olivier acts best when he acts least and that he superbly portrays the dumb agony which the gypsy has in common with his animals.

But universal critical acclaim did not come until very much later in his life and career when, as Lord Olivier, he reached the status of an unassailable national and National treasure. Even his classic film of *Henry V* (1944) was reckoned by Richard Winnington of the *News Chronicle* to be in "overbright technicolor, half an hour too long, at its worst vulgar and obscure" and Mr Winnington found the *Hamlet* which followed on screen to be "intoxicated and sidetracked by decor and deep focus and tracking cameras. It achieves neither first-rate cinema nor first-rate Shakespeare. Olivier could have failed or succeeded more cheaply and more quietly."

Olivier's return from Hollywood and three years in the Fleet Air Arm was to lead to the Old Vic seasons at the end of the war and it was here, in the legendary doubling of *Oedipus* and *The Critic* as in the *Henry IV* and *Richard III*, that critics ceased to regard him as a somewhat dubious interloper from the non-classical world. Olivier's Richard, wrote a fledgling Kenneth Tynan from

Oxford "eats into the memory like acid into metal", a line that deserves to live alongside Harold Hobson's review of a subsequent Stratford appearance ("Olivier's Macbeth is the best Macbeth since Macbeth's").

But it was the savagery of Kenneth Tynan's 1951 attack on Olivier for subduing his Antony until it met the level of Vivien Leigh's Cleopatra ("a cat in fact can do more than look at a king: she can hypnotize him") which was to haunt both players until the moment came when Tynan could be effectively silenced with an office at the National, and no critic ever wrote again of Olivier with such vehemence though Bernard Levin had to note in the *Daily Mail* of David Turner's *Semi-Detached*; "If this is the kind of play which the Director of the National Theatre thinks worth putting on, I can only say that it were better that a Foundation Stone be hanged about his neck and he be cast into the uttermost depths of the sea."

Though his first pre-National season at Chichester opened shakily with *The Chances* and *The Broken Heart*, both of which he directed, it closed with an *Uncle Vanya* (he directed this and played Astrov) which was widely reckoned to be as near perfection as made no difference, and that was followed a year later by the *Othello* with which Olivier crowned his career as Ronald Bryden noted for the *New Statesman*: "The last speech was spoken kneeling on Desdemona's bed, her body clutched upright to him as a shield for the dagger he turns on himself. As he slumped beside her on the sheets, the current stopped. A couple of wigged actors stood awkwardly about. You could only pity them: we had seen history, and it was over."

Twenty years earlier, John Mason Brown the American critic had noted that Olivier was giving performances at the Old Vic "in which blood and electricity are somehow mixed, that pull lightning down from the sky" and nobody after him, not even Tynan, quite managed to capture the essence of Olivier's stage presence. "Pound for pound," wrote one critic of *Titus Andronicus* "he is the greatest actor alive"; and of the career-clinching *Long Day's Journey Into Night* Irving Wardle noted:

a performance of intense technical and personal fascination, personal in the sense that James Tyrone was an actor with the kind of career which Olivier spent his life avoiding: a strong talent destroyed by years of imprisonment in profitable type casting . . . but what marks out his performance most is its breadth: all the components of the man are there simultaneously . . . and there is the sense not only that O'Neill is showing off the different sides of the character, but that Olivier is consciously manipulating them for his advantage.

The critics who best understood Olivier on stage were indeed those who best responded to his animal magnetism: and because of his own gradual conversion to the camera we have, on film and videotape, the best of his work as well as some of the worst. Olivier is the first world-class actor to have been able to leave a permanent record of his work against which reviews can be tested when due allowance has been made for its period and the camera-angles fashionable at the time of recording. Someone soon should set up an Olivier library, where tapes and films could be viewed alongside clippings of original reviews. More often than not, from Oedipus through Archie Rice to Lear, the critic was left gasping as if sent to review a firework display at which all the rockets had been set off at the same moment. In the end, as most of them realised, you just had to be there when Olivier lit the match.

SIMON
CALLOW

SIMON CALLOW

Simon Callow (b. 1949) made his first professional appearance at the Edinburgh Assembly Hall in 1973 in *The Thrie Estates*. He has played in Shakespeare, Brecht, Toller, Shaffer, on the stage, and, on film, most notably and recently in the Merchant-Ivory film of E. M. Forster's *A Room with a View* and *The Good Father*, with Anthony Hopkins. His book, *Being An Actor* (1984) is required reading by young actors.

LAURENCE OLIVIER AND MY GENERATION

When I was at drama school, the Laurence Olivier controversy raged. Was he the greatest actor who had ever lived? Or was he simply appalling, a ham, external, tricksy, unwatchable, and so on? At that time the cons seemed to be winning. It was, in fact, quite hard to find someone to say a word in his favour, among either my contemporaries or his. This being the case, I generally kept rather quiet. I was a *raving* fan, and frankly baffled by the inability of people to see what was as plain as the noses on their faces (not to mention the nose on *his* face, rather larger of course, because generally made of putty): that he was the most exciting, the most daring, most interesting, funniest, most moving performer on the English stage by a mile. It's fifteen years since he was on any stage and nothing has dimmed my memory of a single moment of any performance of his. If an artist's job is to be memorable, Olivier is the supreme acting artist of my lifetime.

The sensuous impact was shocking. Most great actors operate by stealth: one's first glimpse of Ralph Richardson or John Gielgud or Alec Guinness was likely to be disappointing. Only slowly did they weave their spell, drawing you closer to them, luring you to the edge of your seat. It was quite different with Olivier. The initial image was always so clear, projected in bright sharp colours: a voice of symphonic splendour, simultaneously sumptuous and piercing; an aptness of invention; an audacity of timing – and no lack of feeling, contrary to report. In the area where he was supreme master – the tragi-comic – he was desperately moving;

Strindberg's Edgar, Osborne's Archie, Shylock, Richard III – all weasel men for whom at bay he found the authentic cry of pain.

Temperamentally, he was not a romantic actor – despite Heath-cliff – nor a heroic one – despite Henry V. He was a Realist actor, always grounding his roles in a material, observed reality – thus diminishing them in the eyes of some of his contemporaries, who were used to acting in abstract nouns: nobility, majesty, pathos. Olivier was a very modern actor; for all his unprecedented command of the mechanics of acting, his point of reference was not the theatre, but the world. "Acting," he told Tynan, "is the art of persuasion. First you've got to persuade yourself, then you've got to persuade your audience." The all important first half of that requirement was never forgotten, as he nagged away at making sense for himself of every moment, winkling out generalisation, finding the exact parallel. Sometimes the effect was reductive – but whatever you thought about his decision to play Othello black, instead of Nobly Moorish, the way in which he executed his interpretation commanded absolute admiration: he forged for that performance the greatest instrument any actor has ever had at his disposal. The physical, vocal and emotional flexibility of his Othello set new standards for the rest of us to measure ourselves against.

In fact, of course, none of us could begin to match those standards. In his short documentary film, *The Great Ecstasy of Woodcarver Steiner*, Werner Herzog shows how Steiner had entered so completely into communication with his sport, skiing, that he made nonsense of all previous records – to such a degree that he was eventually barred from competing. No one else stood a chance. Laurence Olivier has approached his art like a sportsman or an athlete, and he has won the pentathlon. It was his ambition, he told Tynan, to "fascinate the public in the art of acting in the same way that they might follow a boxer or a cricket player." It was this that lay behind the ritual criticisms of him that I heard so often in my student years: "I can see the wheels going round", "it's all so calculated", "he never moves me", and, again and again, derogatorily, "Yes, it's very clever – I suppose."

It was; it was meant to be. It was also, frankly, intended to annihilate the competition. It succeeded there, too. The *victor ludorum*, the glory-boy of the acting world has, undisputedly, become the Greatest Actor Alive. But this acting that is about acting has proved sterile; it has had no issue. Othello was not the harbinger of a race of super-actors; it was an end in itself. The literalism of the interpretation remained; the giddying virtuosity of the performance flew off the edge of the globe. Nothing was left remarkable beneath the visiting moon.

Every role he played has had to be re-invented by his successors, with only middling results so far. In fact it is acting itself that needs to be re-invented. The post-Olivier vacuum yawns ominously long and large. Many good performances have been seen in the last few years, but there has been no re-definition of the actor's aim. Olivier accrued all the glory to himself; he won all the prizes. If it is not about prizes, and not about glory, what then is it about?

MICHAEL
CAINE

MICHAEL CAINE

Michael Caine (b. 1933) began acting in a youth club drama group, and served in the army, in Berlin and Korea, 1951–53. His first job in the theatre was as an Assistant Stage Manager for the Westminster Repertory Company, Horsham. He appeared in *Next Time I'll Sing to You* at the Arts Theatre, in 1963. A prolific television and film performer he has acted in over 150 plays and films, the latter including *The Ipcress File, Alfie, The Italian Job, Educating Rita, The Honorary Consul, Hannah and her Sisters* and *Mona Lisa*. He starred with Olivier in the film of Anthony Shaffer's *Sleuth*.

THE WHIRLWIND

For me *Sleuth* was a thing that came out of the blue. The first reaction is that I'm working with one of the greatest actors of all time and you accept the part instantly, of course. I didn't expect to get it, and then you're stuck with "What do I call him?" I can't call him Sir Laurence because he's Lord Olivier; basically you're supposed to call him "My Lord", I suppose.

I was pondering this because I'd never met him before the rehearsal – we rehearsed for two weeks – when I got a letter from him and it said, "Dear Mr Caine, it suddenly occurred to me that you might be wondering how to address me as I have a title; well, I think we should introduce us by our own titles which would be Mr Caine and I would be Lord Olivier the first time we meet, forever after that I hope it will be Larry and Michael." And that's how it remained, but it shows the kind of guy he is.

He was in a state for the rehearsals because he had just been fired from the National and I think he was on valium sandwiches; he'd just been ill, and valium affects the memory so he couldn't remember the words, but it was only a rehearsal.

He said to me, "I can't get this guy off, I can't get him, really"; on about the third day of rehearsal he came in and he had a moustache, which was how he played him, and said "Got him!" and the performance suddenly took off. Then you knew he'd found the character. He said, "I'm not like you, you can act as yourself, I can never act as myself. I have to have a pillow up my jumper, a false nose, or a moustache or a wig; I can't do it, I cannot come on looking like me and be someone else like you can."

It was amazing, the transformation. If you saw the moustache on the table you'd crush it thinking it was a caterpillar or something. Suddenly it changed this man into this extraordinary character. It was a bit fraught at rehearsal because there was just the two of us and I remember – I'm always very frank with people about what I feel, most people when they say "I'm frank with people" mean they don't *like* hurting your feelings, that's not the way I'm frank; I'm frank as long as it doesn't hurt your feelings – and so I said to him, "Listen Larry," I said, "you're the greatest actor in the world." I said "I know I can't beat you at this game, but I will never back off. I'll stand my ground." He said "What a wonderful idea, Michael, I'm glad you've thought of it!"

It was just the two of us in *Sleuth*. No one else, and I was the victim. Larry is very much in theatrical terms the actor-manager, so there was in-built in his psyche, shall we say, this someone who was brought along to support his performance, you know, and which *Sleuth* wasn't about. I would never have dared to do *Sleuth* on stage with Larry, but in movies I'd already made twenty-eight or thirty by that time, and he hadn't played a leading role for fifteen years. I said to him one day "You do know you're carrying the movie this time, and someone else?" He said "Yes, it's not easy is it?" I said, "No, I've been doing it for years while you were coming in and stealing pictures with a funny nose and a pullover up your jumper."

Once we had started shooting, which was fine, he knocked on my dressing room door and he said, "Can I come in?" "Yes" I said; he said "I thought we'd rehearse these, but I didn't want to disturb." I said, "I would never disturb you in your dressing room. If you want to see me my door is always open; you just come in, anytime you like."

Wimbledon was on, and I had a television in my dressing room: he said "You've got a television?" I said, "Yes, I'm watching Wimbledon" – it was the year Evonne Goolagong won. He said, "You mean you watch television between takes? Can you do that, what about your . . . ?" I said "No . . ." "God," he said, "I've never thought of it. What a wonderful idea. Do you mind if I come in and watch television?" He was quite astonished at this great brilliant idea that I'd had of putting a television in my room to watch Wimbledon, he thought this was a stroke of genius. He said "Can I come in any time I like?" I said, "Larry, I told you the door's open, you can come in any time you like, because even if I'm changing my trousers it wouldn't worry me. There's no women on the picture. Just come in, watch television and help yourself." He said "You've got stuff to eat and drink here?" His dressing room is absolutely spartan, all he's got is papers and script. I've got everything, cigars, booze, anything you like, not heavy booze, but something to drink like coke. He was astounded at this.

He and I became very good friends because we're opposites. I don't think we were close enough or far enough apart to play practical jokes and also we were in a very intense work situation. He had been sick and ill and in the afternoon he'd get tired sometimes and he'd be doing a take and Joe Mankiewicz* who was directing would say, "Let's stop a minute Larry." He knew it wasn't going right and he'd get angry with himself because he was tired and you'd see him pumping his adrenalin and suddenly he'd start again.

Suddenly – I always remember the first time it happened – out of nowhere came this whirlwind. He is an extraordinary whirlwind, that's the word to describe him. It's almost smothering. It's an extraordinary situation, and an astonishing privilege to witness it. Not like an audience in the theatre, I mean as close as I am, with these eyes and suddenly this genius and fire. Oh, it was extraordinary. I've tried to do it, it usually looks like I've lost my temper. Or I've gone fucking mad, everyone says, "Is he alright?!" It's a kind of changing gear. He goes !!!!!!!! ££££££££ ★★★★★★★★ up in the stratosphere.

He was playing the part of a guy who was acting the whole time. He was acting for me, and then he changed into top. He had these roles; you watch the sequence in *Sleuth* when he tries on the costumes and he's trying to get me into the clown's outfit. That was where the whirlwind came, and the other time was when he started calling me a snivelling slime and all that, because I was crying because he was going to shoot me. That was the other one.

He struck me for all his lordship and genius and everything as being almost one of us without trying or acting to make you feel comfortable – or someone like me, because I'm so patently a

---

* Joseph L. Mankiewicz (b. 1909). American film director (and occasionally writer). His films include *Philadelphia Story*, *All about Eve*, *Julius Caesar*, *Guys and Dolls* and *Suddenly Last Summer*.

working class symbol. I'm not even working class anymore, I'm a symbol, and the way he treated me was fabulous. I'll always be grateful to him. Sometimes those guys can be awful. He shares the same thing with Johnny Gielgud, they are so nice with everyone. But Larry, I don't know how he is in the theatre, I should imagine he's tougher.

He very quickly realised that I knew what I was doing. I see him every now and then and I've had dinner with him, and he's accepted me as a fellow actor, which is an honour. He talks to me as though I'm almost as good as him. He is not someone who can't get the support, he knows that we share the movie, and he's very gracious about it. I don't think that's what he thought he was going to do when he went in, and he's a gracious man.

I saw him the other day in the Olivier Theatre, in the lobby, and I said, "I want to ask you a question, Larry": he always calls me dear boy, "Yes, my dear boy." I said, "Do you get in the Olivier Theatre free?" He said "No, I fucking well pay for the tickets." He was quite pissed off about that; he had to pay to get into the Olivier Theatre. But you can still see that he's getting older, quite frail, and you can still see that sparkle every now and then. His eyes are heavy-lidded and then suddenly it changes.

On *Sleuth* he was so funny, we were in stitches on it. He told me when he was making a film for Sam Goldwyn and he went to see Sam on the day they dropped the atom bomb on Hiroshima. Sam called him up and he said, "You know, Larry, that atom bomb is dynamite!!!" He tells loads of stories like that; remember it was just the three of us, Joe Mankiewicz, him and me for sixteen weeks. Only two of us, so we had to cover everything to make it interesting. We had to shoot it close up, long shot, eyes, nose, fingers, we shot everything around the room, pictures cut to that . . . There's no days off, because everybody was in every scene. It's all one set, it was an extraordinarily difficult film to do.

I remember we talked about money; I said, "Listen, you're out of the National now, so what do you get, about £150 a week?" I said "You can't have any money; stay in movies and don't give a packet what they are, get some money together." And he did; I don't know whether it's my fault he made *The Betsy* or *The Seven Per Cent Solution*. He said, "I never thought of that." I said "What you've got out of it all is a Lordship." I said "I've got several million dollars – you can earn it, they'll pay you for it." He said, "Do you really think so? Do you think I should make pictures and earn a lot of money?" I said, "Of course you should, go out and do it, they can't take the Lordship away from you, they can't take your reputation away from you. You've got a family, I'm not asking how much you earn." He couldn't have been on more than £200 or £300 a week then. I planted the seed of avarice in him.

He had people coming in and out taking letters, because he'd just been fired, there were letters firing off in all directions, and then he'd come in exhausted and we'd watch Evonne Goolagong. He'd always got other ideas. He was always directing himself; he'd say, "Why don't we do this?" and I would either agree or disagree. And if we disagreed, disappear, he wouldn't push it. Then he'd come back with another idea to replace it. Always thinking, always working.

His gifts, I often thought, were for playing kings and the great man, but he did a picture, *The Demi-Paradise*, which I thought was a naturalistic performance in the years before any of us were doing natural, like Leslie Howard used to do. He played a Russian worker who came to England in the war to make munitions: you watch that performance. He's an ordinary down-trodden little guy, not a king at all, and he was born to play kings. I said that once to him; he said, "I certainly wasn't born to play queens, dear." And he was. And his father was a vicar, and he must be a Huguenot. Olivier Protestant Huguenot. Definitely Protestant, quite high church, they would have come when Fabergé went to Moscow.

Johnny Neville looked like Jean Louis Barrault, but Larry talked and had the great voice like Gérard Philipe. Gérard Philipe, funnily enough, was a French Cockney. I knew all those guys. I liked Louis Jouvet. He used to sing because he stuttered . . . He'd say, "*Tout l'art du cinéma c'est de trouver une chaise*." The voice went up and down. He was in the Comédie-Française and one of the students had said, "M. Jouvet, what is the art of the cinema?" and that was his answer: "The art of the cinema is to find yourself a seat – a chair." But you never sit down on it; whenever you sit down on the set you're always sitting in someone's chair, and they say, "You can't sit there."

I'll tell you what, he can knock back a glass of wine. I'm a bit of a drinker, but he'll drink me under, and never get pissed. We didn't used to drink at lunchtime because we had too much dialogue, but we used to go out to dinner after.

His whirlwind with me is the complete opposite. You gradually see the actor disappearing, there's the man there, and I can feel it happening. It's a whole new generation. We were talking one day about our generations, he and I, and I said "When did you first see an actor?" – talking about the differences between him and me. He said "Well, my nanny took me to the local something or other and I sat there and the curtains went up and the lights were bright. Oh," he said, "it was enthralling, that's when I decided to go into the theatre."

He said, "What about you?" I said "Well I went to what used to be called the threepenny rush, on a Saturday morning, which was a children's cinema, and the first actor I ever saw was the Lone Ranger. And," I said, "all my youthful life I lived a quarter of a mile from the Old Vic but I never had enough money to go to it, but I had enough money to go to the pictures twice a week." He said, "That's why you're in cinema." I said "That's right. I'm a cinema person from the day I was born. I'm fifty-three, probably the first generation." A lot of us are fifties, Roger, Sean, Richard Harris, Richard Burton, no Burton was a theatre actor. Richard always used to listen to his own voice; if you talked in mellow tones the way he did, you could hear your own voice in your ears.

PART TWO
THE DIRECTOR

Venus Observed
at the St James's
Theatre, London, 1950.
Drawing by Griff.

CHRISTOPHER FRY

CHRISTOPHER FRY

Immediately after the second world war, Christopher Fry was hailed as the leading playwright in the English-speaking theatre. Born in 1907, he was first a schoolmaster, actor and director before writing *A Boy with A Cart* in 1938 and, in 1950, *Venus Observed*, which starred Olivier. His plays include *The Lady's Not For Burning* (1946) and *The Dark is Light Enough* (with Edith Evans, directed by Peter Brook; 1954). He was awarded the Queen's Gold Medal for Poetry in 1962; his most recent play is *One Thing More or Caedmon Construed* (1986).

COMMISSIONING
VENUS

The first performance of Olivier's I remember clearly was the Romeo of 1935, and I was surprised that the critics found little poetry in his delivery. For me, that slightly crackling sound, flames starting up under a pile of new twigs, set the words free of "tone" to do their own work. What lyricism was lost was made up for by the exact life of the words – of each word as it took its perfect place in the speech – and this, after all, was the truth of the poetry. Even so, for a time I thought his greatest achievement was in comedy rather than tragedy, in spite of the glorious summer of his Richard III (finer in the theatre than on film), which had its being midway between the two worlds, and in spite of the cry of Oedipus which still reverberates in my memory. What could outshine the twin brilliants (alas, I missed his Hotspur) of Puff in *The Critic*, tossing snuff into the air and nosing it down again, and Justice Shallow? Did I really see what I thought I saw, when Falstaff dragged Shallow full tilt from the orchard – Olivier horizontal in mid-air, his feet as high as his head?

But the reservations I had about the tragic roles were cast out by a performance of Othello. No performance of the greatest Shakespearian parts – of Hamlet, Othello, Lear – can be definitive, and here no doubt the "full soldier", the warlike Moor, was lacking, sacrificed to the dark and glowing panther. But a diary entry for May 2nd 1964 records the impact he made on my wife and on me when we saw a matinée performance on that day: "A variety of tone and emotion which gives the full measure of each line – the vibrating merest thread of tone on 'The pity of it, Iago', his face against the wall; the agonising gale that seems to sweep us into 'Farewell the tranquil mind'. It is a fantastically courageous performance, going here and there towards the insane, yet never losing touch with the truth. His final speech when he kneels on the bed with Desdemona upright in his arms is heart-breaking. We came away pulverised." – And later I wrote: "The rage was elemental, the pain so private that it seemed an intrusion to over-hear it."

Fifteen years earlier I had been hammering away at the play he had commissioned for the opening of his management at the St James's Theatre. A slow writer, I had no business to be working to a deadline, and to make matters worse I had interrupted the work to make a translation of Anouilh's *L'Invitation au Château*. In consequence, when I got back to writing *Venus Observed*, I was running late, and working all hours of the day to get it finished in time. It can only have been an anxious time for Olivier. His patience and kindness were remarkable. I have often told the story of how, when things were beginning to look serious, I received a small parcel from him. It contained a typewriter ribbon, far too large for my 1917-model Corona portable, an eraser and a brush to clean the keys. With them was a short note: "Let me know if there is anything else you need, won't you? I'm not making you nervous, am I? I do hope I'm not making you nervous."

At the end of the first reading of the play he asked, very understandably, if I would mind not coming to the earliest re-hearsals, when he would be still feeling his way into it, both as actor and director. They would let me know when they were ready for me. I went instead to the rehearsals of the Anouilh play which I had called *Ring Round the Moon*. I heard nothing more from the St James's. It seems incredible to me now that I didn't just ring Larry and go along. I was far more concerned about *Venus Observed* than with the translation, and I knew that only benefit could come from watching Olivier at work, which would help me to improve those passages in the play which had suffered most from the race against time. How I could have kept away is incomprehensible. I suppose I had got used to attending the other rehearsals, and to go to the St James's, without a definite invitation, would have been like the first day at a new school. It wasn't until the day of the dress-rehearsal that I rang the stage-door of the St James's to ask what time the rehearsal would begin. Olivier came onto the line. "*You're* a funny sort of author, I must say," he said, "never coming anywhere near us."

But what I had missed by not being at the rehearsals was at least partly compensated for by the magnificent letter he wrote to me from New York about his directing the play there, about the casting, and the passages in the script that were difficult to handle, and the New York audiences, and how he had tried to fall in with my wishes in certain points, and the problems that arose in directing another actor in a part that he had played himself – the most vivid account of working on a production that I have ever read – in a handwritten letter three thousand words long. "I told Ruth Gordon about the length of this letter," he writes at the end of it, "and she said that you should give it a title and we should put it on!"

PETER
HALL

PETER HALL

Succeeded Olivier as Director, National Theatre (1973). Previously (for thirteen years) Director, Royal Shakespeare Company when he was responsible for the creation of the RSC as a permanent ensemble and the establishment of a London base for the company at the Aldwych Theatre. Born in 1930, Hall was educated at Cambridge. As well as plays he has directed films (including *Akenfield*, 1974) and opera at Covent Garden, Glyndebourne (where he is Artistic Director), and Bayreuth. He published his diaries in 1983.

THE JOB
HE LIKED BEST

I first saw Olivier act in 1944 at the New Theatre. I saw *Richard III*, *Arms and the Man*, *Uncle Vanya* and *Peer Gynt*. His Richard made an indelible impression on me. When I saw it again in 1947 it seemed to be what Shakespearian acting was all about. Olivier was by then an absolute Protean classical actor. Piecing together what he did in the Thirties from the records, and from conversations with people that he worked with, it is clear that while Larry in his early years was a "modern" actor (resisting old-fashioned rhetoric and sometimes taking great liberties with the verse), he had, by living in Shakespeare, gradually accepted the disciplines of Shakespeare and endorsed them. Shakespeare always wins: if the verse is too chopped up, the part is impossible to sustain.

By the time Olivier did the films of *Richard III* and *Henry V* he was speaking verse in a very flexible, light, and witty manner, and with enormous respect for the form. He has always been a fanatical respecter of the *craft* of acting. There is no actor I have ever encountered who trains more vigorously for a part. He thinks that voice lessons as well as physical training are mandatory. When he played Othello, for example, he decided, like an opera singer, that he had to get two or three lower notes into his voice. He believes that the actor's beginning and end is his own physical prowess. In 1959, I was at Stratford with Olivier and with Charles Laughton. Laughton was doing *Lear*. Larry said to me, "Charlie is a great actor, but he's out of condition." And he was – he had been away from the theatre too long, and he hadn't trained himself to scale one of the great mountains. You can't play major Shakespearian roles unless you are in tiptop condition.

It is Larry's heroic personality, his lion quality, which made him fill out the great parts with such energy and magnetism. A magnificent stage animal, he has clearly always been a performer of genius. But throughout his life he has refined and developed his technique until in his prime he could do anything. He revelled in the fact that in the death scene of *Coriolanus* – in the Stratford production I directed in 1959 – he was stabbed in the belly and fell, hanging upside down from a promontory. He loves extravagant physical feats. In the same way, he revels in showing all the contradictory facets of a complex character. But it is always more a demonstration of a character, something he has assumed, rather than a revelation of himself. Here the comparison with his great contemporary, Ralph Richardson, is illuminating. I don't think Larry ever takes you inside himself as Richardson did. Richardson was in some respects a very Gothic actor – some would say, a very mannered actor. But the poetry of his own soul was completely on display. Larry is an intensely private and many-faceted man. I don't think he exposes himself when he acts. He rather hides by showing you the character he has assumed. He pretends to cry, and will move you by doing so, but he doesn't cry himself. Acting is not imitation but revelation of the inner self. In the final analysis, this is not what Larry does or sets out to do. He is a performer. He does not reveal himself. But he is the greatest of our age – at performing.

My relationship with him during the Stratford production of *Coriolanus* was very close, electric and stimulating. I was twenty-eight at the time and dealing not only with Olivier, but with Edith Evans, Harry Andrews, and a cast of formidable young talent that included Albert Finney, Vanessa Redgrave, Mary Ure and Robert Hardy. People ask, "How on earth does a young director tell Laurence Olivier what to do?" The question misreads what a director is. He doesn't tell an actor what to do; he draws out of him everything he possibly can, and then edits it.

Some time before rehearsals began, I was in Hollywood with my first wife, Leslie Caron. Larry was also there making *Spartacus* – the film he was doing to earn enough money to enable him to work for very little at Stratford the following year. We had many long talks about *Coriolanus*. "All that mock modesty must be cut," he said. "All that stuff about 'Don't praise me,' a sort of inverted Henry V – that must go too. I cut it all in 1937 when I did it at the Vic." I said that the whole point of the character is that he is so proud he can't even bear to be loved or praised; love or praise is a kind of possession and he feels himself superior to it. We sat up all one night arguing this out. Finally the beetle brows settled and he said "I think you're wrong, but you believe it so I'll do it." If you compare the notices of the performance in 1937 to those of Stratford in 1959, you'll see that the critics didn't notice what we'd restored in the text, but they did say that pride and vanity were there in much greater measure.

Shortly after the production of *Coriolanus*, Larry said he was determined to make the National Theatre a reality, and asked me if I would be interested in being his No. 2. With the arrogance of the very young I said I'd love to but that I'd just been asked to run Stratford, so I would do that.

★   ★   ★

The time of the handover to me was very difficult for him and I don't think it is fair to make judgements. It is not easy for anybody to retire. He didn't want to give it up, but at the same time he did – passionately. It was a very contradictory time. I never knew if he was going or staying.

Larry is often seen as the last great actor/manager. And of course he was an actor/manager – he ran theatres as an actor/manager. But he also always has a great historical sense and a great awareness of change. He employed Tynan as a brainbox, and he surrounded himself with fine directors such as John Dexter and William Gaskill and a lot of people from George Devine's Royal Court who were, people thought, antipathetic to him. He was a brilliant runner of theatres, a brilliant man of the theatre, a brilliant impresario, a very great film director, and remains the greatest actor of his generation. It is a formidable list of accomplishments. I don't think he was a great administrator, or a particularly adept politician, but then why the hell should he be? There are plenty of people who can be that.

★   ★   ★

Olivier has been underrated as a film director. For my money, Larry as a stage director was as good as a professional could be. But he had little personality, no "handwriting". In his films, though, the handwriting was plain to see. That he could have made *Henry V* from a standing start as his first film is astonishing. It is comparable with Orson Welles's achievement in doing *Citizen Kane*. The way *Henry V* was shot, the composition, the rhythm of editing, the use of music – it is all very personal, quite extraordinary and altogether revolutionary.

He said to me once that film directing is the best job in the world – better than any other of the things he could do so marvellously. That sense of being able to capture his own vision of how it should be done and how it should be seen, how the audience should look at it, and yet have it for ever, absolutely fascinates him. He seems to me a natural film maker. From the very start, he showed himself the master of beginning a shot and developing it by the movement of the camera so that it made a new and eloquent composition, a new shot – without in any sense making the spectator feel that it was arty or contrived.

The film of *Hamlet* is now a strange period piece, both in its extraordinary cutting and rearranging of the text, and in its black and white look. Colour for *Henry V*, for the panoply and patriotism of England at war, was the right choice. But black and white was correct for *Hamlet*, creating a strange and beautiful world in which Larry's *Hamlet* could happen. Perhaps he was too old to play Hamlet himself. And I don't think he was a great Hamlet anyway – his strength was never for interior men. But it is still a terrific film.

Finally you have to compare the three great actors of that generation – Olivier, Richardson and Gielgud. I have worked with them all and knew them well. Larry seemed to me to be always redefining things in brilliant technical terms – making his art more and more extraordinary and sharp: a dazzling technical display. Ralph Richardson was like a wonderful craftsman, painstakingly carving a piece of wood each night at the theatre and making new discoveries. Out of his craft he made art. Gielgud was an improviser – like a wonderful butterfly he sped all over the place, creating new shapes, new forms and living very dangerously. Their rhythms and their attitudes were totally different. So I suppose finally Olivier was the heroic actor, the man who could display with genius. Gielgud was the romantic actor. And Richardson was the actor who told us about the poetry of people.

JONATHAN MILLER

JONATHAN MILLER

Jonathan Miller (b. 1934) has divided his time between arts and medicine. Educated at Cambridge, he was co-author and appeared in *Beyond the Fringe* (1961–4). He has worked in television (including *Alice in Wonderland*, 1966), and as executive producer of the BBC Shakespeare series, 1979–81. He was Associate Director, National Theatre, 1973–5. He has directed opera at Glyndebourne and for the English National. His books include *McLuhan*, 1971 and *Body in Question*, which was also a television series, 1978, *The Human Body: Pop-up Book*, 1983, and *Facts of Life: Pop-up Book*, 1984.

ABOARD
THE VICTORY O

I first met him informally at parties after *Beyond the Fringe*. He saw the show and was, I suspect, slightly irritated by our Shakespeare sketch. He had sat in a box and it got backstage that he was not conspicuously amused.

My first *professional* contact with him was when Ken Tynan edited a television programme called *Tempo* which was commercial television's answer to *Monitor*. With his wonderful flair for what is fashionable, Tynan had asked us to do a regular satirical spot. In the opening programme this was a pastiche of C. P. Snow written by Alan Bennett, a high table scene of people drinking, wearing gowns and so forth, and bandying conversation about. On the same programme Larry was being interviewed by George Harewood* about the opening of Chichester.

We were on first but we began "corpsing". There were two takes, three takes, and Larry was obviously amused by the fact that the young lads couldn't do it. By the fourth take we could see him getting more and more impatient at these dreadful amateurs. It took something like twenty takes before we got it right, by which time he was thoroughly nettled, if only because we'd kept him waiting so long.

Then I didn't see him for some while, by which time I'd blotted my copybook quite badly with him. When I saw his performance

* The Earl of Harewood (b. 1923), at this time artistic director of the Edinburgh Festival. Later Managing Director of the English National Opera.

as Othello, I told a journalist that while I couldn't help but admire the extraordinary bravura, energy and detail of it, I wasn't all that impressed by the performance as a whole. He was understandably annoyed by this – or I heard he was – and looking back I can understand just how he felt and I'm rather surprised he ever asked me to direct anything. However, some years later I was doing my first and only feature film – an unspeakable catastrophe – and was sitting in the commissariat at Elstree when a message came through saying "Laurence Olivier on the phone". I thought it was Alan Bennett or Peter Cook. Anyway a hoax. I came to the phone and heard this voice saying, "Dear, boy . . . This is Laurence Olivier here . . ." "Joanie wants to do *The Merchant of Venice* and would love you to direct it." No question of him acting in it, no mention of that at all.

I was blushing at the thought of what I had said about his Othello. I would love to, I managed to say and I mentioned doing a nineteenth-century version. He said, "Whichever way you want to." Later I saw from his book that *he* came up with the idea. It may well be that we both thought of it. But, anyway, it then gradually became apparent that *he* was going to do Shylock. Now whether he had thought this all along and had decided to delay committing himself until he found out whether I had an idea which coincided with his own, or one which he could approve of, the fact is that he came to the first reading knowing the part perfectly. Not like the other actors.

This was so characteristic of him. He's very Machiavellian and although this has its drawbacks, there was always something glamorous about his political calculation. It was like working for Diocletian.

Before rehearsals I had a lot of difficulty eliminating ideas of which he had been persuaded by Ken Tynan, who had in turn been persuaded by Orson Welles. The idea, for example, that Bassanio should play all three suitors, including the black one, in order to get the right casket. There was another idea that Portia would present herself in court in a wheelchair. In any case there were a lot of encrustations – Tynan's rather than Olivier's – which I had to careen before I could find the clean lines of the play. Eventually we came to an agreement, which also involved persuading him to drop an enormous amount of make-up – false nose, ringlets, a Disraeli beard, all adding up to a sort of George Arliss. I said, "Larry, please" – (as a Jew I felt embarrassed) – "please, we're not quite like that, not all of us." He then said a wonderful thing. "In this play, dear boy, which we are about to perform, we must at all costs avoid offending the Hebrews. God, I love them so." "The best way to do that, Larry," I said, "is to drop these pantomime trappings which are offensive and unnecessary." He agreed to drop the ringlets.

But he had invested in extremely expensive dentures which gave him this strong prognathous look (based, I think, on a member of the National Theatre Board), and he was so attached to them in both senses that I felt I would have been a terrible spoilsport to object to them. He used to go round the corridors of the National Theatre seeing whether anyone knew he had them in. He would give interviews to journalists wearing them. He loved them so much and he looked rather good in them – and I couldn't bring myself to object!

In the event we did a lot of horse-trading. I would give *him* ideas and he would exploit them. He never tried to push rank. He has what all really great actors have – an expedient recognition of good business. If you have a good idea he'll take it from you regardless. If not he will go on to "automatic pilot", or rather he'll take over the controls himself.

I suggested the little dance, at the moment when Tubal tells him Antonio's ships have gone down. I also suggested that he entered baring Jessica's dress in his arms when he discovers her flight. This reminded the audience subliminally of Lear and Cordelia – another father "betrayed" by his daughter. I suggested his crying at the end, though not in any way which he didn't utterly make his own. He always looks for a memorable effect at some critical moment and I remember him saying, "Oh God, I've done a fit, a fall, I cannot possibly fart!" I said, "Why not try humiliated, terrible crying. *I* can't do it, but I know *you* can." Off he went and gave it this curious unparaphrasable energy and vehemence which did actually freeze the blood. I remember him saying, "Oh dear boy," and there was a look of brimming gratitude in his eyes. He has an absolutely wonderful, really humble magnanimity. If something is good, it doesn't matter who or where it comes from.

When *The Merchant* opened I became aware of his stage-fright, as he called it. I didn't know it was that, not until three or four days into the run. He certainly never spoke about it during rehearsals or run-throughs or on the first night.

I was standing in the wings one night and could see, in that rather unnatural light coming from elsewhere which you see from the darkness of the wings – a look of shocked terror on his face, beads of sweat on the make-up and his eyes staring as if they were behind a mask. I couldn't detect anything more than a hesitation. I knew, though, from brief moments of stage-fright in *Beyond the Fringe*, that what to an outside observer seems like a thirtieth of a second is half an hour for the victim. He then confessed to me that he had these moments of appalling, shattering lapses in which he forgot his words and the earth stood still. There was a night when he actually forgot the things that a Jew has. "Hath not a Jew eyes? . . ." One was almost tempted to say, "Hath not a Jew elbows!"

After the event he was wonderfully humorous about it, but I should imagine from the drenched and exhausted way in which he came off-stage it was far from funny. It think it happens to a lot of people as they get older. It was obviously more than mere forgetfulness. It was the terror of a moment of standing outside himself and seeing himself suspended in the night sky of a theatrical performance, illuminated by all those lights, watched by dimly visible faces – and frozen. It must have been a horrible experience.

But he seemed to recover from it because far from retiring as he threatened to do, he came back with redoubled vigour in *Long Day's Journey Into Night*. He has this curious and startling immortality, which became part of his charisma. He would be fatally ill one moment and the next moment he'd be back on stage doing a part of heroic length with some superbly accomplished piece of business, giving the performance of his life. Everything about him as a public performer is to do with being unexpected, unpredictable – Machiavellian in fact.

His ability to shift with the tide is also absolutely astonishing. There was a time when, despite the noble glamour of his roles in *Henry V* and *Hamlet*, he belonged, for a lot of younger people, to another era. The slightly clipped tones, the romantic, matinée idol, nothing whatever to do with us, and we all thought he was yesteryear. Then quite suddenly he was doing Archie Rice with brilliant modern seediness. He took on the very thing which denied everything he *had* been. In place of the glossy, beautiful, noble, grand creature of earlier days, he was suddenly scratching the inside leg of his awful check trousers as a seedy comic, offending all the ladies who had adored him. He renewed himself in this act of metamorphosis – a sort of phoenix performance. It's part of his

Above: Fabia Drake's *Twelfth Night* picture with, on left, Olivier as Maria, centre, Fabia as Toby Belch. Below: part of Olivier autograph letter to Fabia Drake.

Telephone: TEMPLE BAR 3878.

MEMO. ... BOX OFFICE.

NEW THEATRE

ST. MARTIN'S LANE,
W.C.2.

Oct 29

Fabbie my prescious

First of all to thankyou once more for the lovely black away the beautiful telegram, but mainly for all your angelic solicitations throughout this trying time. You realy are an angel to write me that lovely letter. They were horrible weren't they? But I'm ever so much cheered now and feel much better for everyone going out of their way to

Early studio shot, 1935, with lemur (Angus McBean).

Mercutio in 1935 (Angus McBean).

Above: With Michael Caine in *Sleuth*, 1972. Right: Big Daddy in *Cat on a Hot Tin Roof*, 1976.

Left: in *The Ebony Tower*, with
Toyah Wilcox and Greta
Scacchi. Below: Lord
Marchmain, asked for a final
confiteor by Father Mackay,
Nial Toibin, in *Brideshead
Revisited*, 1981.

With Joan Plowright in *Daphne Laureola*.

Machiavellian strategy. Be unexpected, come back as something else. If they think you're dead, spring to life; if they think you're passé change your course. Identify with the enemy, join them, and then beat them. No one else could manage to be as Protean, as Machiavellian, as self-serving – and remain so lovable.

Those of us who knew him as a father, as a leader of the National Theatre, saw he had what he had always wanted, as a great patriotic Englishman: control of the whole show. He was always the great commanding officer. He would have loved to have been the captain of the flagship which sank the *Bismarck*. He always wanted to serve his majesty and there he was, in command of this grounded boat, fifteen brass rings on his sleeve and a bridge of his own.

The very set-up of the National, the offices in Aquinas Street, were like Pompey's galley, or like the shacks on those HMS training ships which are on land. It was absolutely made for him. Whatever competitiveness he might have had among his peers, was now sublimated into running his ship. Dispensing largesse, interest, and patronage to younger actors. His eminence had been recognised and a lot of otherwise competitive energies were turned to totally benevolent purposes. He loved the thunder of feet on the Companion Way. He was always speaking down the tube, lots of clang clangs to the engine-room, backings and churnings of propellers, and people brought up unexpectedly to the bridge. He had genuine interest in the welfare of his staff, like a first class captain on a battleship. "Sign on. Everyone is expected to do their duty." And because of this he created an enormous competitive admiration and filial affection amongst those who worked for him.

DEREK
GRANGER

DEREK GRANGER

Derek Granger (b. 1921) was a drama critic and a literary editor before becoming a distinguished producer of television programmes, including a series with Laurence Olivier which he here describes. In 1981 he produced for Granada Television Evelyn Waugh's novel, *Brideshead Revisited*, which was highly acclaimed on both sides of the Atlantic. Laurence Olivier played Lord Marchmain.

THE GRANADA FACTOR

It was an unenviable stroke of fate which led Laurence Olivier to make his unforgettable contribution to British television. Although in the 1950s he had made appearances on the American networks in Somerset Maugham's *The Moon and Sixpence* and Graham Greene's *The Power and the Glory*, his furiously dedicated director-ship of the National Theatre had devoured far too much of his time and energy in these later years to leave any to spare for television.

The suggestion eventually came from his brother-in-law, David Plowright, the managing director of Granada Television. The proposal was put to him at his bedside in the Royal Sussex Hospital, Brighton, where he was slowly recovering from his third serious illness within a decade. This time he had been struck by a particu-larly rare and unpleasant disease which had brought him very close to death and now left him with the horribly debilitating condition of a general muscular wastage. He was at a point when his life was at its lowest ebb – hopelessly weak and exhausted and with no prospects of work for months ahead.

This was the opportunity that David Plowright seized to issue his invitation: that Larry should come up to Granada in Manchester as soon as he felt strong enough and produce there a series of twentieth-century plays entirely of his own choice, and to be made under his total supervision.

It is fascinating how the qualities which mark the work of great actors are those that also reside in their own private character.

Olivier's genius derives from an extraordinary and mysterious combination of ruthless bodily and mental energy, a commanding and powerful physical presence, a compellingly handsome actor's mask and the ever-present communication of a nerve-tingling sense of danger. These are the qualities of the true hero and it is that amalgam that has equipped him so superbly to play the kings and princes, lovers and black villains of dramatic literature.

Never had he needed those qualities more than at this moment, or realised so absolutely that it was on his own reserves of resolution, courage and defiance that he now must draw. If Plowright had suggested his plan as a form of therapy to keep him buoyant during a long convalescence, Larry now rose to the idea as a new challenge, requiring every ounce of energy and concentration that he could muster.

In the spring of 1975 Larry was discharged from hospital in time to spend his sixty-eighth birthday at home in Brighton, and if the celebrations were necessarily somewhat muted at least he could now begin thinking positively of the formidable labours ahead.

So it was that in the following long and hot summer he started work in his secluded Sussex hideaway – a charming extended row of flint cottages (once the local Malthouse) lying snugly between the Sussex Downs and splendid open water meadows stretching away to the east.

My own part in this exercise requires perhaps a brief explanation. I had been recruited by Granada to help share the burdens of production partly because I was an experienced old hand who had worked for many years in Granada's play department, but also because I had worked closely with Larry in the National Theatre's Old Vic days when I had done a three year stint as literary consultant. For Larry and me it was a working reunion.

We would sit in the garden shade with the plays of the century strewn about us on the grass – Shaw and Granville-Barker, Rattigan, Coward, O'Casey, R. C. Sherriff, Clemence Dane, Bridie, Osborne, Whiting, Pinter. Larry was quickly enraptured by the work of Harold Pinter. He relished both his language and that very special cunning which creates such perfectly marked spaces for the actor's art to fill. James Bridie's *Daphne Laureola* was another clear favourite, not least because it had been one of his most notable ventures into theatre management. He had first presented the play with Edith Evans (who had created in it one of her most famous roles) almost thirty years earlier.

Osborne's daring play of *fin-de-siècle* Vienna, *A Patriot For Me* (up to that time only presented in club performances at the Royal Court), was also high on the list. In the meantime, in the shade of the mulberry, we continued the debate. If it was to be Maugham should it be *The Circle* or *Our Betters*? Which play from Miss Horniman's sturdy Manchester School, *Hindle Wakes* or *Hobson's Choice*? And which American plays should we include? Was *A Streetcar Named Desire* the best representation of Tennessee Williams; was the beguiling *Morning's At Seven* by Paul Osborn a better choice than weightier drama by Arthur Miller? Were we sufficiently balancing comedy and drama, were any of our favourites likely to be available?

At lunchtime we picnicked and mulled over our reading, and in the late afternoon took a break to swim in Larry's new pool. Here, on each successive evening, he had set himself a new target of laps, for he had now become a dedicated swimmer and believed no other exercise would restore his weakened frame more quickly.

During those relaxed, companionable days Larry grew ever more active. When I arrived in the morning he was invariably engaged in gardening or domestic chores, trimming the hedges, starting a new miniature plantation, attempting a most ambitious example of topiary in the shape of the Three Sisters and generally presiding over his country estate as if he had recreated for himself an off-duty character from Chekhov – a nice mixture of Astrov, Firs and Sorin. So passed some of the happiest working days of my life and as that splendid summer began to wane, he finally decided on his first selection: *The Collection*, *Hindle Wakes*, *Saturday, Sunday, Monday*, *Daphne Laureola* and the first two American plays, *Morning's at Seven* and *A Streetcar Named Desire*.

In the early autumn he made a special trip to New York in his new role of a television producer raising money for a most expensive series. It had been decided to make his chosen American plays as co-productions with an American network and it was the network president himself who hosted the inaugural luncheon at which Larry quickly charmed a large table of heavyweight tycoons into a state of absolute surrender.

It seemed an agreement had been reached. That at least was the verdict of our huge, enthusiastic and happily married agent, Gary Nardino, who had become so excited by the outcome that over a celebratory glass of champagne at the 21 Club he declared emotionally: "I love that guy so much if ever I go gay I'll ask him to elope with me.'' And as Larry started preparing for *Marathon Man* – his first major film part since his illness – in countless meetings with agents, lawyers and accountants, and with Larry deftly steering things his way, the deal was slowly hammered out.

Tennessee Williams's *Cat on a Hot Tin Roof* was proposed instead of *Streetcar*, not only because it was less familiar but mainly because in Big Daddy it contained a thumping great part for Larry himself. The first rumble of opposition came when the idea of *Morning's at Seven* received a less than rapturous welcome. A hapless executive, whose computer had predicted a lack of viewers because the play was largely devoted to the problems of growing old, began to sound increasingly inept, particularly as Larry had been enlisting a cast which was to include Jack Lemmon, Walter Matthau, Katharine Hepburn, Myrna Loy, Henry Fonda and himself. He received the rejection in grim stony-faced silence, and I felt that the poor executive could detect behind that basilisk stare the suppressed frustration of Othello, Richard III and Henry V combined.

Larry's visit to New York had inevitably turned into an almost royal progress. Having booked lunch at a famous hotel restaurant I noticed that not only had the hotel manager turned out to greet him but the hotel owner himself. At a party given by his old friend and American agent, Milton Goldman, great names of the film and theatre world – Lillian Hellman, Martha Graham, Irene Selznick, Lillian Gish, Douglas Fairbanks – had foregathered to meet him, while other stars of equal magnitude waited humbly to make their obeisances. Personally the most down-to-earth and unpretentious of men, Larry is also the last person in the world to be conscious of status. He now seemed oblivious of his power to compel awe. His private preferences are closer to those of an old campaigning soldier who likes nothing better than to relax and reminisce with old cronies. Here in New York he diligently sought out old colleagues from the National Theatre such as Frank Dunlop and Jeremy Brett and made strenuous efforts to track down a young staff director who had once assisted him at the Old Vic.

Once over a long late supper with Garson Kanin and Ruth Gordon the discussion fell to the delicate question of whether an actor should ever take a drink before going on stage. Ruth Gordon confessed that a good swig before going on could sometimes make for a fine entrance. Larry, heartily admitting a love for drink, took the view that discipline was all when work was the priority, concentration was impossible without absolute sobriety and that his habit was often to give up alcohol as soon as he began rehearsals. Larry has always possessed the precious gift of intimacy, relishing the give and take of personal disclosure and the exchange of confidences, the wilder and the saltier the better.

He also possesses an intense human interest in other peoples' lives. It was characteristic of him to discover that the pianist in his hotel cocktail lounge was an ex-actor and, between the entertainer's sessions, sit with him swapping stories of provincial touring; and typical of him to disappear into the Algonquin's lavatory to be discovered ages later in deep conversation with the elderly Lithuanian attendant on the problems of coping with another people's language.

Larry was now not only committed to his plays for Granada but also to *Marathon Man*, with John Schlesinger as director, which was scheduled to start shooting immediately. The following twelve months were to provide as strenuous a convalescence as any invalid ever undertook. In the two years following his illness he not only produced six plays for Granada, as well as starring in five and directing the sixth (*Hindle Wakes*), he also took on film roles in *Marathon Man*, *The Boys from Brazil*, *A Bridge Too Far*, *The Jazz Singer* and many more. Altogether, between 1975 and 1981 he acted in a total of twenty films.

★   ★   ★

The Granada project began in earnest in the spring of 1975. I marvelled at that driving and unsleeping will which enforced an overwhelming need to be always the unchallenged leader. There was no means of persuading him not to take charge of everything.

The world of television provided him with a new toy, a tempting box of technical gadgetry and special effects which he now had to master and control. It also fed his obsessive interest in every detail of production. He took to it with immense vigour. He pored over design plans and ransacked London and Manchester for locations; he designed his own titles and supervised the complicated "opticals" which ensure each credit remains on screen for exactly its allotted time; he chose and helped compose the title music, suggesting to his young composer some variations on a theme which he had used to open the Festival Theatre at Chichester; for the main title shot he climbed stoically to the top of a derelict high-rise office block and kept a chilly vigil on the roof, taking

137

film-camera pictures of a ruddy Manchester sun setting behind
Granada's studios. He auditioned (with a wonderfully warm and
sympathetic courtesy) actors and actresses for the smallest of
supporting roles; he moved tirelessly between cutting room and
dubbing studio, between rehearsal room and film location; and he
largely adapted his own play texts, ruthlessly editing them to
television length by the simple empirical process of himself reading
aloud most of the parts, claiming this was much the best way to
discover the boring bits.

Those of us around him were amazed at the uninhibited and
un-neurotic zest with which he embraced all his new activities.
Ken Tynan, at the National Theatre, had once said that if ever
he were given one word to describe him that word would be
"turbulent".

We also used to speculate on what he might have become if not
the leading actor of his generation – a controversial archbishop, a
great general, a commercial magnate, an Admiral of the Fleet? He
seems not to need that choppy passage between thought and deed,
that element of brooding reflection which afflicts most creative
artists. The axiom he remembers as having most impressed him
in his youth was uttered by the lecturer who pronounced: "The
best way of preparing yourself for anything is to do it."

★   ★   ★

The first of Larry's Granada plays to go into production was
Pinter's *The Collection*. Alan Bates, Helen Mirren and Malcolm
McDowell joined him to form a superb cast and the brilliant young
Michael Apted (an ex-Granada trainee) was assigned to direct. An
indication of Larry's rehearsing method was supplied by Michael's
slight twinge of alarm after the first few days' work. Larry,
playing the role of the ageing couturier Harry Kane, whose young
companion (Malcolm McDowell) is suspected of having an affair
with an attractive dress designer (Helen Mirren) had chosen to
present the fullest portrait of the character as early as possible.
Michael was worried that there was too much overlay of manner-
ism and detail and that the feminine elements of the character had
become too emphasised. What Michael failed to realise, perhaps,
at this early stage was the absolutely sure, protective instinct which
urges Larry to take the most startling lineaments of a character and
with those physical characteristics – the look, the walk, the stance,

the voice – create the whole edifice of a different personality. It derives from that fierce imperative which always goads him onwards: Never be boring. Even at a first reading he feels the necessity to startle and arrest.

Larry, sensing Michael's reaction, called me: "I think our young director is displeased." I made soothing noises and, as gently as I could, persuaded Michael to bide his time. Miraculously, the excrescenses were quickly shed. What emerged was possibly one of his finest and most haunting later performances. One moment of it was marvellously created in rehearsal. It is the passage where Kane breaks down in front of his young companion's accuser (Alan Bates) and which Larry had already been rehearsing as a moment packed with poignant feeling. Now he suggested that he should try it again, this time with the emotion suppressed, the pain concealed, as of a man desperate to keep his self-control. The transformation was electric, the scene infinitely more powerful. But he was still not satisfied and wanted to try again. The next time he would attempt the scene with the emotion banked down but would allow himself a small crack in the armour. From beneath the icy matter-of-factness there came a sudden breaking of the voice, from which issued a sudden, stifled sob of quite heart-rending effect. The great key moment of the play had been brought to a pitch of perfection. It was extraordinary to see the moment take its shape in that dusty, bare rehearsal room.

For *Cat on a Hot Tin Roof* he had assembled an especially starry cast including the bewitching Natalie Wood (to die so tragically, a few years later), her husband, the ever-youthful Robert Wagner, and that powerful but vulnerable actress, Maureen Stapleton.

Robert Moore, who had made his reputation with the plays of Neil Simon, was the director, which pleased Natalie, who strongly believed that with a grounding in comedy he was better equipped than most to undertake the melodramatic resonance of Tennessee Williams's play. The rehearsals went happily, with Larry doting almost paternally on Natalie and Robert Wagner, a long and very close friendship which meant much to him. But there came a point when the director, baffled by what seemed to be Larry's strenuous efforts to depict Big Daddy in as despicable and repellant a light as possible, confided to me his unease. The scenes which puzzled him were at the beginning of the play. Big Daddy, reprieved from his cancer attack, confesses to his son, Brick, how he intends to celebrate his victory over death by going with the ripest whores of the town. Robert Moore was dismayed at the grotesque relish with which Larry was communicating his libidinous intentions and fearful that such gusty "tastelessness" might alienate the audience.

His worries were those of a man who felt he was in some way acting as guardian over a national idol and who was fearful that the idol would merely arouse disgust. Yet that was precisely Larry's intention – he was deliberately emphasising this sudden on-rush of elderly lechery not only as a proper expression of the life-force naturally reasserting itself after the threat of extinction, but as the actual starting-point for the audience's slow discovery of Big Daddy's character, the eventual grandeur and nobility of his decline. At the end of the play Big Daddy, after his short reprieve, dies painfully, after he also becomes reconciled to his alcoholic son – a scene in which he shows great reserves of compassion and perception. The misunderstanding over Big Daddy's grossness was an apt illustration of a creative process, carefully thought out and deeply felt.

Rehearsals continued in a new-found amity and understanding, interrupted only by a hair-raising occurrence when Larry's ferocious schedule took him away for several days to complete his scenes in some remote location in Holland where he was playing the elderly Dutch doctor in the film of *A Bridge Too Far*. As inevitably happens the film scenes greatly overran their allotted time, and he was only delivered to Granada's studios after much anxious telephoning to airports and car firms – and with a last desperate dash across the lowlands to catch his plane to Manchester, where shooting was to begin within the next few hours.

"I don't feel very well, I haven't slept all night" he confessed, shortly before launching with enormous vigour and zest into Big Daddy's volcanic row with Big Mamma at his birthday party – one of the most taxing scenes of the play.

Bridie's *Daphne Laureola* was the next play of the series, with Joan Plowright resplendent in the role of the eccentric Lady Pitts and Larry very delicious in the role of her aged and infinitely understanding husband.

The comparatively light work-load imposed by Bridie's comedy was followed by the gruelling intensity of William Inge's small-town American drama *Come Back, Little Sheba*, about a pair of misfits imprisoned in a hopeless marriage. The magnificent Joanne Woodward played the pathetic Lola, mourning for her youth and her lost dog, Sheba, while Larry, undertaking yet another of his extraordinary physical transformations, now became Doc, the mid-Western chiropractor fighting to stay sober in the shadow of alcoholism. It was another enormously exhausting, emotional role and Larry hurled himself into it with immense passion, rehearsing time and time again, and with unabated energy, the final scenes.

By this time my own part in these productions had become somewhat superfluous. The small help I could offer in such matters as the arranging of studio schedules and the choosing of crews, was hardly necessary any more in view of Larry's insatiable appetite for the technical side of production – indeed, his zest for technicalities finally led him to take over both production and the direction of that delightfully sturdy example of the plays of the Manchester School – Stanley Houghton's *Hindle Wakes*, for which he directed both the film and the studio sequences, bringing a finely calculated home-spun realism to Houghton's study of Lancashire mill-town morals in 1912.

The delicious little cameo role of the old Italian grandfather in Eduardo de Filippo's Neapolitan comedy *Saturday, Sunday, Monday* rounded off the Olivier series for Granada, but this was by no means the end of an interest. For Thames Television he gave his memorably touching portrait of John Mortimer's blind barrister in *A Voyage Round My Father*; again for Granada there was the sensual old painter of John Fowles' *The Ebony Tower* and the marvellously witty, poised and sardonic Lord Marchmain in *Brideshead Revisited*, a role to which he brought an undiminished glow of authentic glamour.

The great peak of his achievement in television was still, however, to be reached. Since working at Granada in the seventies he had dreamt of doing *King Lear*. That dream was finally realised in 1982 in a performance, finely directed by Michael Elliott, which seemed miraculously loaded with the qualities of his own temperament and humanity, an extraordinary and touching fusion of the greatest of Shakespearian roles with the greatest of all English actors.

It was fitting that Larry's brave adventure into television, undertaken as a way of fighting his way back to health, should have resulted in this supreme achievement. Once again in his career, the reward was universal acclaim. That recognition was nicely crowned when, after a special showing of *King Lear* at the White House, the President of the United States told him: "After that performance I don't think I'll call myself an actor any more."

PART THREE

THE MAN

Peer Gynt, New Theatre, London, 1944. With Ralph Richardson as Peer Gynt.
Drawing by George Stampa.

DOUGLAS
FAIRBANKS JR

DOUGLAS FAIRBANKS JR

A long-standing friend of Olivier, Douglas Fairbanks Jr was born in 1909, the son of Douglas Fairbanks Sr, famous as a swashbuckling, acrobatic film actor. Douglas Jr's films include *Little Caesar* (1930), *Dawn Patrol* (1931), *Prisoner of Zenda* (1937), *Gunga Din* (1939) and *The Corsican Brothers* (1941). He has also starred on the British and American stage and produced innumerable films for television. He served in the US Navy and, as well as action awards from his own country, won the British DSC. He was made an honorary KBE in 1949. He visits Britain frequently but lives in the United States.

BLUSHING HONOURS THICK UPON HIM

Have you ever had a close friend with whom you shared jokes and plans and disappointments, or just plain idle times; with whom you sang or grumbled, or compared preferences in people and places and anything else that came to mind; with whom the harmony of silence was as agreeable as the playing of childish pranks or discussing the wagging of the world? And then have you seen that same friend at another later period who so marked his time as seemed now to bestride the clouds high above the crowd, so removed from you and us by reason of his new outsized renown, by "that divinity which doth hedge" a star celebrity, someone so blown up to larger-than-life proportions that some wondered if anyone *that* exalted ever so much as sneezed, had an itch, went to bathrooms, or knew at first-hand some of the problems (and pleasures?) of lesser mortals? And then, after all that, have you tried to reconcile the latter fantasy with the former fact by realising that both were one and the same person that you see one way, and the world sees another? It could be not unlike an Ancient Greek looking up to Mount Olympus, seeing Zeus and saying, "Dammit, we used to be just 'people' together once. *Now* look!!" Well, that's *almost* the way I sometimes feel about Laurence Olivier.

What can I say about him that has not been more eloquently said before and will, with increased verbosity, be said again? Were I to try, he no doubt would laugh and accuse me – in rightly bawdy terms – of an ill-fitting sycophancy.

Frankly, I couldn't tell you – without quoting my betters – how I would grade him professionally, as an actor, a director, a producer (or *even* as a make-up artist specialising in noses!) I have a blind eye and a deaf ear insofar as my friends are concerned. Before I go to see and hear them, I have already brain-and-emotion washed myself so well that, for me, they can do no wrong. As far as my professional friends are concerned, I must frankly admit I'm a very poor critic. However, meanwhile, I am told by those who *do* know, who are both responsible and honest, that Laurence Olivier is really one hell of a great actor! Many informed people may, for their own and reasonable reasons, rank others as his equal. A few might well place others such as Gielgud, Scofield, Jacobi, Johnny Mills, or Albert Finney in this category. Perhaps. And maybe McKellen or Sher or Mastroianni. What about American actors, not necessarily classical. Hoffman? Possibly. Or Newman? Al Pacino? Redford? de Niro? Canadians, Hume Cronyn? Or Christopher Plummer?

And don't forget the dead, but not forgotten by many of the living: Richardson, Burton, the Barrymores, Chaplin, Forbes-Robertson (too far back, perhaps!), or the Europeans, Werner Kraus, Jean-Louis Barrault, *et al*. The more remote Orientals – like the great "classical transvestite" Mei Lan–Fang? Opinions differ considerably and deservedly. But none deny Olivier's place on the "shortlist"of the best. And most of his contemporaries put him at the top, at least in the "English-speaking" category.

Yet, on the other hand, before his courageous dedication to high-quality classicism replaced the temptations of great wads of money for becoming one more popular face I remember him well as an ordinary mortal – and extra-ordinary friend. It was at a time when we were both usually "between engagements". Sometimes we'd go fishing, or sit up in restaurants singing lusty songs in different languages which neither of us understood. (If our voices were untutored, we did have equally good ears for alien accents.) Once, as some friends and I were on our way down to fish off the Mexican coast from a chartered sailboat, we anchored near a little Indian village to wait for Larry to join us. He was arriving in a tiny putt-putt plane from Los Angeles – a long and slow trip in those days. We thought it would be robust "Ho-ho-jolly" fun to have him arrested on arrival, so I went and made a deal with the old boy who was the sort of local mayor. He was as big as a house and full of tequila. The so-called mayor was immensely amused and sent four unmatched Indian *gendarmes* down to meet his plane and fine him *20,000 pesos*! His "crime" was being an Englishman. Larry kept saying, "Where's Fairbanks. Where's so-and-so, etc . . . ?" They shrugged. Larry protested, "I want to see the British Consul!" They shrugged again, saying, "We no recognise Britain." Then they left him to stew for half an hour in an awful gaol. When they let him out and he discovered what we had done, instead of being angry, he thought it was all terribly funny and doubled up with laughter.

This was at a time when we were both in California and when Hollywood producers referred to him loftily, whenever they referred to him at all, as that "rather nice but stiff-necked Englishman with a French name who looks like a young Ronald Colman" – and that was about *it*. In spite of a well-travelled intelligence accompanying a contagious and bawdy good humour, he was always absolutely, and uniquely, dedicated as an actor. As all even just good, ordinary actors are, he loved – and still loves – being "someone else". To assume the looks, manners and sounds of others than himself – and then take on whatever "himself" is.

Going back and forth across the Atlantic, and sometimes even further afield, he relentlessly built up an impressive list of the best and most versatile acting credits around. To do that and not inspire excessive jealousy (to be sure, he begot envy – but never of a vicious variety) required an awareness of his own expertise, plus understanding and patience! And there was – probably still is – an unspectacular, quiet, "un-exhibitionist" facet to him. For example, there was a day – nearly half a century ago – when he, David Niven, Robert Coote and I were all together in a boat off Catalina Island in California. It was the day war broke out: September 3rd, 1939. Niven, as an ex-professional British Army officer, took off within days intending to rejoin his regiment as a subaltern in the HLI. Coote joined the RCAF in Canada. Laurence Olivier said nothing then about his own plans. He was involved in movie commitments from which he couldn't legally extricate himself . . . although he *did* hint he'd return to England as and when he could. But to do *what*?

I had known from various jokes we'd exchanged that he *hated* flying, shivering at the thought of it whenever he had to travel by air. At the time he was obliged to be at his studio, usually between seven-thirty and eight o'clock every morning. What he actually did was to get up at, say, five o'clock every morning and, without telling anyone, except a few intimates, he quietly took *flying lessons*! His teeth may have been chattering like dice in a box, and his knees cracking together like Huntley & Palmer biscuits, but he *did* it – and without any fanfare! In due course, he finished his film assignments followed by a too-brief, ill-fated postponed promise of a North American tour of *Romeo and Juliet* (with his more or less bride, Vivien) and then returned to his beleaguered homeland. By that time France – indeed most of Europe – had fallen to the Nazis; Russia was still allied to Hitler, and Olivier's country was standing alone – *all* alone – against the still-conquering Nazi hordes. When relatively young Laurence arrived home (he was already over age for British conscription), he was able to present himself, and get accepted as a qualified pilot in the Fleet Air Arm of the Royal Navy. And that was when he joined his friends "once more into the breach . . ."

When, years later, he had conquered almost every professional world there was to conquer (including stage and film director-producer), he was laid low with one desperately serious illness after another, and his days had been mournfully counted by pessimistic physicians. It was then he decided the best way for him to counter the debilitating effects of the treatments he had been taking was by acting in the most difficult and most strenuous play he could find – Strindberg's *Dance of Death* – and to tour it around Great Britain and across the US and Canada. But that's just another facet of the kind of fellow he is! *We'd* call it "gutsy"!

If there's any easy way to success – real, *lasting* success, in *anything* – reflect a minute on the fact that over the last fifty-eight years, Olivier is listed as having acted in well over one hundred plays and over fifty movies, and God knows how many TV plays, . . . so far! That doesn't count what he has directed and/or produced! Such talent, however immense, neither flowers nor survives without the nourishment of strong resolution, self-mastery and just bloody hard work behind it! As a result, he has borne, as had Shakespeare's Cardinal Wolsey, "his blushing honours thick upon him". Foreign governments and institutions have festooned him with awards; his colleagues have garlanded him with even more; and his own monarch created him a "parfit gentil" knight before he was forty years old, thus becoming Sir Laurence (or, as he preferred, Sir Larry).

Then, years later, after the Queen's then First Minister twisted his arm, he hesitatingly accepted the first peerage ever granted to an actor – a profession once derisively said to be composed of mountebanks (some say it still is!) – and so, subsequently, he became a baron – and known as Lord Olivier.

But then he received one of the rarest among Britain's honours: the Order of Merit which ranks second only to the Order of the Garter. It is the personal gift of the sovereign and is limited to, I believe, only twenty-four members in the world at any one time. Men like Dr Schweitzer, Lord Mountbatten, General Eisenhower, Rudyard Kipling, Solly Zuckerman have received it – so you have an idea. Now *Olivier* has it.

But he not only receives recognition for his multiple accomplishments as an actor of the theatre, and the screen, and as a director and a producer, but he *sometimes* dispenses honours himself. I speak authoritatively, as I am *one* of his beneficiaries. In fact, it's one of the most self-esteeming honours to which I can aspire; he has named me his friend – and has done so for over three score years.

As we are now praising just *one* famous man, let us, with others of his friends and colleagues, review, look upon and cheer the life of one Baron Olivier of Brighton, OM, once Sub-Lieutenant Olivier RNVR (A), better known as Laurence Olivier, more familiarly known as Larry.

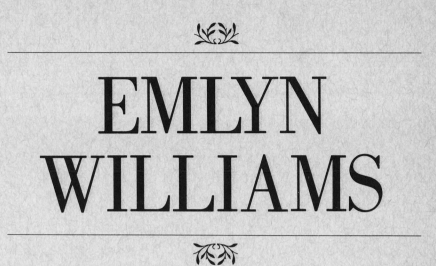

EMLYN
WILLIAMS

EMLYN WILLIAMS

Emlyn Williams (b. 1905), playwright and actor. His plays include *Spring 1600* (1934), *Night Must Fall* (1935), *The Corn is Green* (1938), *The Light of Heart* (1940), and *The Wind of Heaven* (1945). He is renowned for his one-man performances of Charles Dickens and Dylan Thomas, and is the author of two outstanding early autobiographies, *George* (1961) and *Emlyn* (1973), and of *Beyond Belief*. This is his eightieth birthday tribute.

BRIEF ENCOUNTERS

1935, June the 17th, 3 am.

"I'm washed up – I'll never make it!" I can hear it now, a mutter of despair, in the Lyons Corner House in the Strand, more anon . . .

1949. I was sitting in the stalls of a Broadway theatre, where Josh Logan was auditioning young actors for chorus-work in *South Pacific*, most of them six feet or over. After one boy, not quite so elevated, had sung his bit, the director called out, "May I ask how tall you are?"

The young man drew himself up and gave his answer, rather coldly. "Mr Logan, I am the same height as Sir Laurence Olivier."

Well Larry, I thought, all those fourteen years ago, you were wrong. You *have* made it . . .

★   ★   ★

"Mr Williams, in your time you seem to have acted with them *all*, Gielgud, Richardson, Ingrid Bergman, Gary Cooper – tell us, what is Lord Olivier *really* like?" (Or Sir Olivier, or Lord Laurence, it depends on which American talk-show I'm on) . . . "What? You've *never* worked with him?"

I never have. As can often happen, he and I once acted in the same film without ever meeting, not even on the set, not even in the restaurant: *David Copperfield* (1969), described with a shrug as "the movie with everybody in it". I played mad Mr Dick, and

Larry was the sadistic schoolmaster Mr Creakle. The two charac-
ters never coincided.

We have known each other, however, for fifty-one years. During all of seven years before that first meeting in 1935, I had been
aware, as a fiercely ambitious novice in the theatre, of another
equally fierce novice who was steadily doing better than I was.

In 1928, aged twenty-two, I returned from my first job, a small
part in *And So To Bed*, on Broadway, dreaming dreams of being
a playwright but with the immediate necessity to get work as an
actor, in "character-juvenile parts". Realistic enough to face the
fact that for me, as yet, the West End was out of bounds, I
concentrated on seeking a goodish supporting role in the inevitable
"Number One Tour" of any current London success, which
venture entailed a preliminary tour of the Theatrical Agents. Two
separate office-girls advised me to apply for a free seat for the
Drinkwater comedy *Bird in Hand*. "They might favour you on a
Monday, 'ave a squint at a small part, the girl's sweetheart, played
by . . . Can't remember the name . . ."

Gerald Arnwood . . . Laurence Olivier. It was indeed a small part,
attractively treated by a boy with darkly romantic looks and an
interesting stillness; there was a composure in him, unusual in a
generation of toothy over-eager young actors acting young. Can
hindsight analyse the effortlessness as having bordered on indiffer-
ence? Did it mask mild contempt for a bland assignment felt by a
youth with his eyes firmly focussed on the top of the ladder, and
with – in his twenty-year-old mouth – the taste still of the leading
parts recently savoured at the Birmingham Rep? The sharp heady
tang of blank verse . . .

I thought, if he can be darkly romantic at the Royalty Theatre,
Soho (the West End!) I can do the same at the Grand Blackpool,
but I didn't get the part. After six months up and down agents'
stairs, I informed myself that dark romance was not for me, and
lowered my sights. Back to Olivier.

★   ★   ★

Six months after my visit to *Bird in Hand*, I ran into my old Oxford
friend John Fernald; he was off to a rehearsal. "Only a Sunday
show, I'm stage-managing, help me with these props, will you?"

I took one of his parcels. In Poland Street, Soho, I followed him
up to the usual bleak rehearsal room. At the far end, two young

actors were at work on a death scene; one knelt on the grimy floor while the other sprawled awkwardly on three kitchen chairs. "Interesting play," John whispered loyally, "but too special for week-days, they always are, damn it . . ."

The two actors turned out to be Maurice Evans and Laurence Olivier, the play R. C. Sherriff's *Journey's End*. Its sudden blazing success was to land Olivier in a quandary: would he plump for a London run in this marvellous starring part, or be seduced by Basil Dean into playing an even more marvellous starring part, at His Majesty's Theatre, in a spectacular *Beau Geste*? He shut his eyes and joined the Foreign Legion, an adventure which spluttered miserably away after a few weeks. *Journey's End* ran for a year and a half. Bad luck.

Then years in the public eye, with varying success; he was up and down like a yo-yo, mostly up. *Paris Bound*; on Broadway in *Murder on the Second Floor*; a supporting part in *Private Lives*; a success in *Biography* with Ina Claire; a success with Marie Tempest in *Theatre Royal*. I caught an occasional fleeting sight of him hurrying into or out of the Arts Theatre Club, looking – with a wisp of a Ronald Colman moustache under a black Anthony-Eden homburg hat – as if he were playing a faintly Satanic Lothario imperfectly disguised as an Under-Secretary. My climb up was being slower, he was out of my ken.

*   *   *

1935, June the 17th, 3 am (as anticipated above).

My new play *Night Must Fall*, after a rocky three weeks' tour, when it had nearly died of starvation ("Who wants a murder play without a mystery?"), had opened in the West End two weeks earlier and was – to compound bragging with a cliché – "the talk of the town". The management suggested a midnight matinée, so that any actors who had the same daytime matinées and were interested, could see the play. *Any* actors? They all came. (Forgive my blowing my own rather dusty trumpet.)

"Now come on," you may ask, "is this piece about Laurence Olivier, or about *you*?" Point taken, here he comes again.

For he attended the midnight matinée. Alone. Also in the audience was John Buckmaster, accompanied by a twenty-two-year-old girl who, a month before, had made a resounding success in *The Mask of Virtue*. It was one of the first times, if not *the* first, when in an interval – Larry found himself in conversation with Vivien Leigh.

After the performance, my wife Molly and I ended up (around three am) at the last resort of sitting-up Show-Biz: the Lyons Corner House in the Strand, tea and poached eggs or kippers, with my leading lady Angela Baddeley and her husband, Glen Byam Shaw. With us, "latching on" as he put it, was the most depressed human being, for his age, I had ever seen. Sad, sardonic, without hope. Larry.

He was obviously pleased, for us, by the success of the play, and – as he candidly confessed – envious. "One consolation" – a sudden characteristic twinkle – "I see from *Who's Who In The Theatre* that you're eighteen months older than me, and always will be." "Except," I said, "that by the time we're seventy the gap will have shrunk." The idea of either of us reaching eighty was, of course, inconceivable.

We tried to cheer him up, to no avail. "I'm washed up, I'll never make it . . ." It was incredible. Then he reminded us that during the last couple of years, he had been slipping. "Hollywood just didn't want to know, Garbo turned me down for *Queen Christina*, *Ringmaster* was a flop . . ." A month before, within a few days of Vivien Leigh's triumph, he had gone into management with a play called *Golden Arrow*, starring himself and introducing a new young actress, a gorgeous red-head who had stolen the play from under him: Greer Garson. "I had a dull part, but people said I was dull in it – and now there's talk of me alternating Romeo and Mercutio with Johnnie G., imagine me speaking verse next to that one, I'll sink without trace . . ."

(In 1987, when young actors have one eye – often two – on television, it is not easy to recall that fifty years ago the London theatre was the only field in which a straight British player could hope for conspicuous success. Which meant that failure in the West End was much more serious than it is now. That night, Larry looked as lost as an abandoned orphan who has stumbled into a deep puddle.)

But the orphan picked himself up and dashed away the tears. Romeo did draw the strictures he had feared, but Mercutio restored confidence, slowly but surely he climbed the ladder which was to waft him to dizzy heights. I only wish I had a video-tape of that Corner House night, so I could show it to any promising young actor in the dumps about his career.

⋆　　⋆　　⋆

August 1958.

After a five month tour of Australia, for me a Sunday with Molly at Notley Abbey was a most welcome change of pace. A group of friendly and amusing personalities – David Niven, Margaret Rutherford, Van Johnson, Coral Browne – basked in the garden sun and in the warmth of Vivien's beauty and high spirits. It was impossible to think of her as a woman in her forty-fifth year; this was an ageless sprite, mischievous, glowing.

Were the spirits *too* high? Not for the guests, whom she utterly captivated, but for her husband, possibly . . . (hindsight again) too mercurial?

His manners were as impeccable as they were sincere; he greeted each of us with a genial smile. Niven was in great form, and the outrageous Hollywood stories evoked the old Olivier chuckle . . . But in between his participation as host, did the light, without ever going out, seem to flicker? After a time, unobtrusively, he wandered off into the garden, which he loved, and from where I sat I could see him bent solicitously over plants I knew nothing of: a solid country squire who had never set foot on any stage.

Did our distant chatter and laughter sound a little hollow? When he returned for the lively luncheon, his subdued smile gave nothing away. The only clue to abstraction was the occasional steady look at his wife, as she talked and laughed and held irresistible sway. He looked then, for a few seconds, watchful, even anxious – and then he would shake himself free and chat effortlessly to one of us.

Perfect behaviour, and we all had a perfect day as the guests of two fascinating people.

⋆   ⋆   ⋆

March 1959, six months later. Hollywood.

I was playing in a Los Angeles theatre and staying with Larry and the Roger Furses⋆ in a little hill-house overlooking Sunset Boulevard; he was playing a subsidiary part in the film *Spartacus*, with Kirk Douglas in the name part. Charles Laughton was also in it. The star of *Henry V* and *Hamlet* was not happy. "In between

⋆ Roger Furse (1903–72). Stage designer, also closely associated with Olivier's films: the costumes of *Henry V*, *Hamlet* and *Richard III*; also *Spartacus*, and *The Roman Spring of Mrs Stone*, one of Vivien Leigh's last films (1961).

ordering me about, they remember to smack me on the back and remind me I'm the greatest British actor of the age, I don't think Charles likes it very much . . ."

The night of my arrival (he was not working next day) he gave a party for me, a high-powered enjoyable bash which went on for hours – hours which got smaller and smaller. Next day – no, the same day, twelve noon – my host and I found ourselves alone on the terrace, drinking coffee. After the noisy turmoil of the night before, the silence of the empty house felt strange. We talked of the party, of the occasional awkward moments and verbal clashes which enliven a good Hollywood get-together, and Larry was at his funny best.

Then he said, suddenly, "When do you go back to London?" I told him it would be in a couple of weeks, from San Francisco. Then he said, "I want to talk to you about Vivien."

It was startling. Molly and I had, of course, heard from friends, after the nightmarish European tour of *Titus Andronicus*, that things were "not going well", but I had felt I did not know Larry anything like intimately enough to broach the subject. Since my arrival, I had purposely avoided any mention of Vivien, and this was totally unexpected.

"I know how fond you and Molly are of her, and you'll be seeing her when you get home, won't you – well, will you do something for me? Will you try to convince her of a fact she is refusing point-blank to accept? The fact that I am leaving her."

Then he did indeed "talk about Vivien". I was face to face with a floodgate, opened for a moment by an inch or two, with the pent-up flood escaping in spasmodic painful spurts. I knew, somehow, that at that traumatic time, Larry must be unburdening himself to close friends, and I felt touched and gratified that he should now turn to me.

He talked of their first years together, of the delirious mutual obsession: then of the slow and insidious infiltration, into their idyll, of her mental illness, a disorder which, in the fifties, was to most people frighteningly unfamiliar, and for which there seemed no cure. He spoke, jerkingly, of nights when, groggy with over-work, he had been catapulted out of precious sleep, back into the ravelled sleeve of care – into nightmare. He spoke of the immense strain of opening performances made even more unbearable by the hovering possibility of disastrous public breakdown: of his love turning first into acute distress, then transforming itself, tragically, into pity, and helpless pity at that. Then the vain frantic attempts to control the ungovernable by appealing, cajoling, bullying even. Then, coming out of utter exhaustion, the appalling sensation of love turning to murderous hate, and the futile attempts to stop that happening . . .

The quiet voice (had it really filled theatres, and cinemas too?) stumbled on. I looked, from the tormented face before me, down over the smog-shrouded capital of Make-Believe, a place to which we both carried life-long passports . . . but at this moment, the hunted creature before me had nothing to do with simulation – no telling pauses, no sudden artful outburst to betray that the quietness had been a preparation for the outburst. Here was a tragedy stripped of heroics; this was a man pleading that he had been through hell, and would stay haunted by the experience. It has been said of Laurence Olivier, as indeed of many lesser players, that in real life "he never stops acting". If he had been acting that morning, who would have sensed it more quickly than another actor?

No, those were the agonised eyes of a deeply sensitive human being trapped in an age-old and hideous dilemma – the man who, irretrievably and through no fault of his own, finds himself out of love, but is bound with bonds that can only tighten, until he suffocates. A sufferer at the end of his tether.

As I listened, my distress on his behalf was intensified by my concern for poor benighted Vivien, because I knew that her immense strength of will went side by side with a dangerously morbid fragility, utterly dependent – in between crises – on what she called, at moments of truth, "the love of my life" . . . I could see that that fragility must inevitably create, in her husband, continual unreasoning pangs of guilt. It was an impossible situation.

His talk to me that morning clearly stemmed from a craving for relief: the relief of confession. It was to make me understand perfectly something he did years later, something for which he has been criticised: he finally decided to put it all on paper, and to publish it. An act of exorcism, bold but salutary.

★　　★　　★

The years sped by. As often happens when two actors travel busily all over the world but never in the same company, Larry and

I would exchange affectionate but hurried greetings at official functions, parties and (most often, I fear) at Memorial Services – "I take it you're still eighteen months older than me?" . . .

Corfu, the summer of 1972, I was living in a tiny villa which Molly and I had built, on a hill overlooking the sea.

Larry suddenly arrived, a fugitive from the National Theatre, for a couple of weeks of peace and quiet, with his family: his wife Joan Plowright and their three children. They were staying in a family bungalow on the beach in front of the Miramar Hotel along the coast. After a week, they came to spend the day with me.

I walked down the path to the coast road where the taxi would drop them. They were a minute early, and walking towards me in the hot holiday sun.

I shaded my eyes and watched them as they climbed, in a leisurely file. They were all relaxed to the point of laziness, a sandalled brow-mopping tourist group with the same word "holiday" written all over them, escaping from bad weather and city pressures: two pretty little girls, a roly-poly schoolboy who would fine down later, a holiday mother, young and pretty, placid humorous eyes reverting watchfully to her charges.

And fifthly, drawing up the rear, the head of the house: a sedate retired bank-manager, the salt of the City, his conventional off-duty garb a concession to the Mediterranean sun, a *pater familias* at peace after the wear-and-tear of other people's overdrafts, under his arm the invisible airmail *Financial Times* purchased at the village kiosk. You would guess that the only time the gentleman ever entered a theatre was when annually he marshalled the children into a box for a Yuletide treat of *Peter Pan*; the idea of that bespectacled face having ever been subjected to greasepaint and false whiskers surrounding a series of false noses, was utterly untenable. In Corfu, we were not too far from where King Oedipus once lived and died; but the cry of despair which had once chilled audiences to the marrow, was a million miles away.

I led the family up to our terrace, where they . . . relaxed. Bathing togs, inflated playthings, coca-colas, then a stroll down the garden to the sea. As we crossed the coast road, we passed a family of tourists who looked identical to my guests, and the two groups exchanged the fleeting glance and polite smile of the English abroad. No second look – "What did you say? . . . A well-known *London* actress?" – and even the retired bank-manager had escaped detection. He didn't seem to mind a bit.

Tea on the terrace. Then the children found their own fun up and down the garden (mother ever watchful, there was a swing), and we three settled for ouzo and talk of mutual friends and the London scene. Larry tried to remember the name of a girl who had acted with him in *After All*, in early 1930; I got up and fetched, from the bound series on a bookshelf, the *Play Pictorial* numbers for that date. "I was a year old," murmured Joan, directing a glint of mischief at us both. Her husband smiled at her, benignly, over his spectacles.

Turning the pages, I came upon *Private Lives*: a full close-up of Gertrude Lawrence and a rather caddish-looking young man with black brilliantined hair and the old Ronald Colman moustache. Both were looking into the camera, he with a stare which popular "lady novelists" used to call "a veiled look".

"Good God," said Larry, "look at that rosebud mouth, the photographer obviously touched it up, disgraceful . . ." Joan said nothing. "And," he went on, "they'd spelt my name wrong!" The caption read VICTOR . . . LAURENCE OLIVER.

I looked at him. For a fleeting moment, the retired bank-manager cum *pater familias*, had ricochetted back into the ambitious young aspirant to eminence in the theatre: fiery, sensitive, vulnerable.

Then the children raced up the steps from the garden and asked Mummy if they could have some ice-cream from the fridge. Mummy said they could, and Daddy sat contentedly back.

Happy birthday, dear Junior.

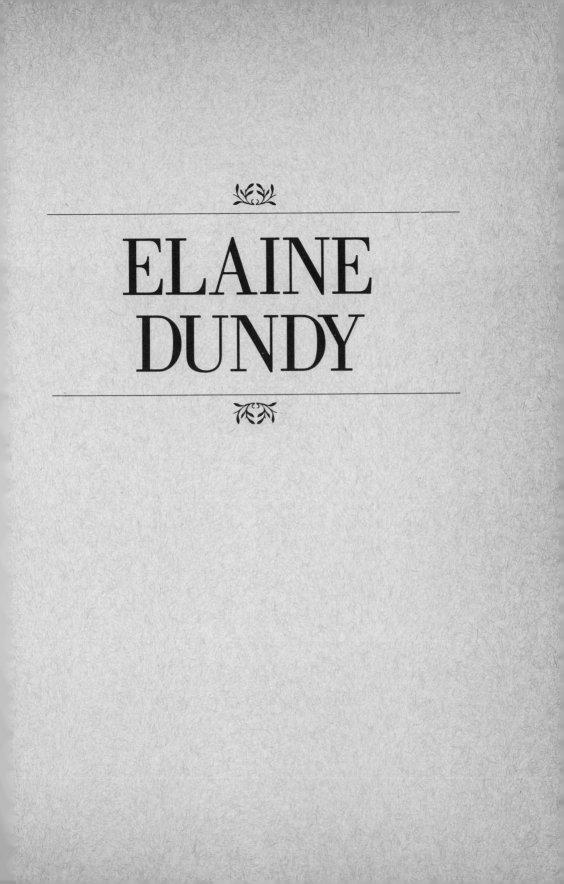

ELAINE
DUNDY

ELAINE DUNDY

Elaine Dundy was born in New York and studied painting before she became an actress. She lived in England for nearly fifteen years and was married to Kenneth Tynan. The author of three novels (including *The Dud Avocado*), most recently she has published biographies of Peter Finch and Elvis Presley. She now lives in California.

NOTLEY ABBEY

In the winter of 1958 Natasha and Peter Brook invited us to dinner at their house. On arrival I was surprised to find Laurence Olivier and Vivien Leigh. It was the first time either Ken Tynan (to whom I was then married) or I had ever met them.

There were no other guests. At dinner the talk was general, everyone participating, everyone, to my astonishment, appearing at ease. I say to my astonishment because some time back when the Oliviers had performed in *Antony and Cleopatra*, Ken had devoted a long article in the *Evening Standard* to attacking Vivien for not adequately partnering Olivier. It was his passionately held opinion that Vivien's Cleopatra was not up to Olivier's Antony, forcing him to stoop to accommodate her. This article had caused a great furore in theatrical circles provoking Noël Coward, no less, to wave an admonitory finger at Ken while informing him that, "It sounded as if Vivien had snubbed you at a cocktail party." We heard tales of Vivien's deep hurt and Olivier's towering rage. More recently, Ken had continued highly critical of Vivien's acting whenever she shared the stage with Olivier.

Yet now at the Brooks' all seemed forgiven or forgotten or cast aside.

I was dazzled by Vivien's beauty. The closer one came to her physically, the more beautiful she was. Her face had a kind of delicate carving so fine-grained you couldn't see it at a regular distance; the kind that was caught forever in her film close-ups.

In contrast, Olivier, appeared solid, almost stolid. Nevertheless

I found myself in a state of excitement sitting next to him for all through my growing up the image of Heathcliff had been my most potent romantic fantasy. Now I found when I looked into his eyes they were such deep tunnels I got lost in them.

I took away from that dinner how civilised the Oliviers were and how charming. As for Ken, it set him up for weeks. He had met his idol, the English actor he worshipped above all others. And his idol – contrary to rumours – had not punched him in the face.

Not long after, Vivien invited us to dinner at their house. It was just the four of us and it was as pleasant and without strain as our first meeting had been. This time Vivien impressed me with her formidable intellect and her knowledge of art, literature and philosophy. Describing herself as a Zen-Buddhist Catholic, she told us she would soon be visiting the latter day saint Padre Pia in Italy before going into rehearsal for Giraudoux's *Duel of Angels*.

My first novel had just been published and Olivier congratulated me adding, "I won't read it. I've never read a novel in my entire acting career except for *Sister Carrie* because I was going to be in the film of it." With this pronouncement I became aware of Olivier, the actor-manager so devoted to his calling he read only for work; never for pleasure.

Olivier and Ken stayed on safe grounds of theatre abroad.

To my surprised delight Vivien telephoned me when she came back from Italy. We began lunching together.

The Vivien I lunched with at restaurants such as the Connaught was elegant, cool and possessed. Then I took her to a little out-of-the-way Thailand restaurant. It was full of Thai students. Slowly at first, then in ever increasing waves, they came to Viven for autographs. Suddenly she became tense and distressed and her body began to tremble and her hands to shake. Finally, in a barely audible voice, she said to them, "Please let me eat." I could have kicked myself for letting her in for this situation albeit unknowingly.

While Vivien was playing in *Duel of Angels*, Olivier was filming. They were on different time tables (so, in fact, were Ken and myself at this point of our marriage). While Olivier went to bed early to get up early, Vivien unwound after 11 pm curtain with late night supper parties.

I hadn't heard from Vivien for a while when I read in the papers that Jean Giraudoux's *Duel of Angels* was temporarily closing to allow Vivien to rest. Hers was a long, demanding role, I knew, on stage almost for the entire play, but she had seemed to me to thrive on it.

Then I remembered something I'd completely forgotten: some years before Vivien had had a much publicised breakdown so severe that it had necessitated her leaving a film in mid-shooting. But surely that was long past. Now I remembered her face pale and tense as she tried to control her hands while signing paper napkin after paper napkin for the oncoming rush of Thai students.

Then Vivien rang me and invited me to Notley for a weekend. She would be sending the car for me on Saturday morning. Notley Abbey! Like everyone in or out of the theatre I'd heard all about the fabulous, magical Notley. Now I would actually see it with my own eyes.

On Saturday morning there was a complication. Vivien's invitation had not included Ken (Olivier would not be there either) but Ken wanted very badly to come along and implored me to ask Vivien if he could. This posed a dilemma. Though she'd sounded fine over the telephone, Vivien was presumably in fragile health. Was Ken the critic (and Vivien's harshest one at that) the ideal house-guest for her to be entertaining? Yet the two times they'd met they'd gotten along well. I rang Vivien and with apologies asked if it would be all right if Ken joined us. Yes, said Vivien. It turned out to be quite a weekend; not least because two unplanned arrivals would strike off each other a light that would become the flame of each one's future.

We arrived that beautiful sunny summer day at Notley. Vivien greeted us wearing an organdy full-skirted dress; a large brimmed straw hat with a blue band hung down her back.

Notley's main halls were dark, baronial and imposing. But upstairs were the prettiest bedrooms imaginable, light and airy where the eye glanced with pleasure at whatever it discovered; some delicate china figure or a book that Vivien had specially placed on the bed-table knowing it would interest a particular guest. Among the other guests was a man I shall call Bill (who was to turn out to be on the Oliviers' staff), and Vivien's mother.

Vivien was in high spirits. It was just the day for a picnic and the picnic was held on the grounds near the river. With our picnic food we drank a lovely dry white wine that tasted like flowers.

Vivien, animated and vivacious, was holding forth. A wasp began buzzing around her. Suddenly the charming Scarlett O'Hara became the harrowed Blanche du Bois. Her face went rigid with fear, her hands flailed the air. She shrieked "Go away! Go away!" at the wasp. Shivering, she buried her face in her hands. Bill wrapped a shawl around her shoulders and held her for a moment. When she took her hands away from her face, the wasp was gone and all was well again. I saw that I had finished my glass of wine. Someone poured me another. I drank deeply.

After the picnic I walked back to the house with Ken. He had never seen Vivien upset before and the effect on him was curious. He walked slowly. He yawned. "I'm sleepy," he said bewilderedly. "I've got to have a nap." Back at the house Vivien showed Ken to a room where he could sleep without being disturbed. Then we all went to the croquet lawn but Vivien had begun to argue with her mother. "You're to blame," she cried. "It's all your fault. You never wanted me to play Blanche. You tried to stop me."

"Vivien, behave yourself," said her mother, to her forty-five-year-old daughter.

Now clocks were playing tricks with time and it was tea-time. The other guests had apparently departed and Vivien had gone to wake up Ken. I was sitting in the grand baronial hall alone with Vivien's mother having tea. "I'm so glad Vivien has you for a new friend," she was telling me. "She needs intellectual stimulus. There's nothing the matter with Vivien, you know. She doesn't need all those psychiatrists. She really loves me. Why, as a little child at the convent, the nuns told me she loved me so much she used to cover up my photograph with her blankets every night so my picture wouldn't get cold." Somehow I found this tale of extreme filial devotion rather chilling. At this point Bill came in. Alarmed at Vivien's behaviour he had contacted Olivier in Spain where he was on holiday with his beloved brother who was dying of cancer. Olivier was flying back. "We'll wait dinner for him," said Bill. "I'll be staying on too." He turned to me apologetically adding "I'm afraid with the extra people there won't be much to eat."

I wonder now that it didn't occur to me at this point that it would be better if Ken and I left promptly. I can only say it didn't. Instead I went back to our room and fell asleep.

When I awoke Ken was sitting on my bed dressed in chain mail armour. He explained that it was the original chain mail Sybil Thorndike had worn in the first production of Shaw's *Saint Joan*. Vivien had awakened him and made him put it on. I told Ken about Olivier coming and he took off the chain mail and we got dressed for dinner.

Vivien, stunning in a red and gold sari, served us sherry. "Larry is coming back tonight," she said. "Ken, put Sybil's chain mail back on, it always makes him laugh."

While Ken was upstairs Vivien took me over the grounds to see her "folly". Vivien's folly was an alley of cypress trees she had planted with a fountain in the middle. As she led me through it in the darkening twilight it seemed to me that the silhouettes of the trees were turning into men in evening dress. Then, as the breeze stirred them, they became Scarlett O'Hara's Southern suitors at a ball bending and stretching towards her, imploring her for a dance. She showed me Olivier's folly too. It was a serpentine walk of hazel trees on one side and lime on the other which ran down to the bank of the river. The walk was known as "The Walk Where You Will" and Olivier used to learn his lines pacing its solitude.

Some time later Olivier arrived. I can still see the long candlelit dinner table in that huge dark dining hall. Way up at one end was Vivien in her sari with Ken sitting next to her in chain mail. I noticed that it was miles too long in the sleeves for him, they dribbled over his fingertips and made it difficult for him to eat.

Way down at my end of the table I was seated between Olivier and Bill. I noticed that Vivien's mother had stayed over too.

As I had been forewarned, there was not much to eat though the food was doled out to us very grandly indeed and stately wines flowed freely, changing from course to course. I realised however, I could not just sit there silently guzzling.

"How was Spain?" I asked an unsmiling Olivier, idiotically.

He let the question go. "How's your book selling?" he asked instead.

"Oh, great."

"When it makes enough money we can run away together and you can support me." As he said this I felt a kind of anger coming off him as though he were demanding that I rise above the awkwardness of the situation and respond to him, flirt with him, *anything* to keep up my end of polite dinner chit chat.

"Oh, sure. Yes. Ha-ha." I said, or something like it, and as before, became lost in the deep tunnels of his eyes.

After dinner we retired to the study. In the ever expanding and contracting Notley household there now seemed to be only four of us: Ken and myself and Olivier and Vivien.

Over the brandy Ken suggested we play a word game. And though we all played it for a while I was, after the brandy, clearly not up to the concentration required. Doubtless Vivien sensed this for she said, "Come with me Elaine, I know a better game than this."

Vivien and I went up to her bedroom where, seated at her dressing table, we began splashing ourselves with her various rare and expensive perfumes. Then we went downstairs to another room and we had some more to drink. We listened to records. We danced. We giggled a lot and just generally behaved like tipsy schoolgirls.

When we finally returned to the study Ken and Olivier were deep in an intense discussion while Vivien's mother, bolt upright, sat mute on a sofa. Ken had abandoned his chain mail and, for the first time since we had arrived, was relaxed. As for Olivier, he seemed a different person. While Vivien and I had been cavorting elsewhere it seemed clear to me that Ken and Olivier had struck up some chord of harmony and that it had released an energy in both of them. Playfully I perched on Olivier's lap for a moment wondering as I did how Vivien's mother would react to her new "intellectual friend". She didn't. Soon after, the party broke up.

Next morning dawned grey and drizzly, fitting right in with my hungover condition. I asked Ken what he and Olivier had been talking about so intently last night.

"An English National Theatre," said Ken in an awe-struck voice. "It's not just a some-time-in-the-future project to Olivier; he wants to be the head of it and he's taken steps towards it. He's talked to a lot people." Ken began to stammer in his excitement. "H-he's d-done a l-lot of p-planning. He wanted to know what I thought of it." Now the stammer became rampant as he recounted telling Olivier that a National Theatre for England had been his most cherished dream. "No one else c-can make this happen but L-Larry," Ken said exaltedly.

Vivien came into our room bearing a breakfast tray of tea and toast and soft boiled eggs; an exquisite vase held a single rose. "Larry wants you to take a walk with him when you're dressed," she said to Ken. Minutes later Ken was ready.

I, myself, was still dressing very slowly when Ken returned. I saw from his face that something bad had happened.

"Larry's kicked me out," he announced. "He wants me to leave immediately. He says I'm having a bad effect on Vivien. She's having one of her spells. Apparently she's had them for a long time and they're cyclic but he told me that ever since that piece of mine appeared in the *Evening Standard*, the cycles have become more frequent. He wants you to leave too. Well," he took my hand and attempted a smile, "you're my wife. I'm sorry. Really." We looked at each other and I knew we were on the verge – as we had been so often that year – of making it up again.

"You behaved better than I did," I said. "At least you didn't get drunk."

"I was too scared."

"I was scared, too," I said, and began packing.

We would, in fact, return the next Sunday at Vivien's invitation and in Olivier's absence at which time we listened to Noël Coward records and Ken held Vivien's hand and they both wept.

But a seed had been planted that chaotic night as Olivier sat talking in his study to Ken about his vision of a National Theatre however little Ken's presence there was then to his taste. It was a seed that would grow into an obsession with Ken until by the mid sixties he was where he wanted to be: working at Olivier's side as the National Theatre's Literary Editor – that is, the man in charge of reading, judging, selecting and promoting plays old and new in their repertory, as well as prodding Olivier to act in such personal triumphs as *Othello* and O'Neill's *Long Day's Journey into Night*. And was it not Vivien, the most directly wounded, who by her forgiveness of Ken had brought them together?

173

ANGUS McBEAN

ANGUS McBEAN

Any illustrated record of the theatre of the 1940s and 1950s will inevitably contain photographs by Angus McBean (b. 1904). For almost two decades he was the foremost theatrical photographer of the day. Most West End plays, especially those presented by H. M. Tennent Ltd, were recorded by his camera. All the leading actors and actresses sat for him, but he first began photographing Olivier well over fifty years ago, after a disastrous first encounter.

PHOTOGRAPHING LAURENCE OLIVIER

It is not easy to those outside the profession to know actors in any real sense, and a photographer, although he may specialise in stage work and spend long hours in the theatre, is not truly *of* the theatre: he is just a subsidiary worker called in to do a special job. Like a plumber or an electrician, and also, let's admit it, something of a nuisance, holding up rehearsals and dragging out whole casts the morning after a gruelling first night in Manchester.

However he does see a different side of the stars, especially if he is lucky enough to be the chosen favourite photographer of the star he is working with – a precarious position I was fortunate enough to hold with Laurence Olivier for some thirty-five years at the height of his remarkable stage career.

Of course I have told the story of my first disastrous meeting with Larry before, but I think it will bear retelling. It was in the early thirties and I had lost my job as an assistant in Liberty's at a time when there were no jobs, and, being stage-struck, I was trying to be an odd jobs man in the theatre. During this time I had the great good fortune to meet the three girls, stage designers who called themselves Motley.* I had even done a number of jobs for them – masks for Ivor Novello, shoes for John Gielgud. My press-cutting book starts with a programme for *Richard of Bordeaux* . . . shoes by Angus McBean! But I hadn't had much work from them for some time and the wolf was sniffing round the door. So

* Sophie Harris, Margaret Harris and Elizabeth Montgomery.

177

one Saturday afternoon I decided to go to see them at their St Martin's Lane Studio; I might even get a cup of tea; but, alas, they were away and only George Devine,★ newly down from whatever college and filling in time working for them as a general dogsbody, was there and with him a young man in a mackintosh crouching over the fire. I was introduced, but didn't take much notice; tea seemed definitely to be over and George, whom I never thought liked me very much, making conversation, asked me whether I had seen their new play. It was *Romeo and Juliet* and Motley had done the designs. "No" I said, "I am waiting for John to take over as Romeo." There was a moment's silence and then the young man by the fire shot to his feet and, in a swish of his mackintosh that failed to cover long tights and a glitter of gold, wrenched open the glass doors and said over his shoulder, "Well goodbye – I must get back to the theatre," and was gone, clattering down the iron staircase from the studio.

"My God, that must have been Olivier," I said appalled.

"Indeed it was. Not your afternoon is it, Angus?"

Now I suppose I should explain that John Gielgud, producing, had arranged that Olivier would open as Romeo while he, Gielgud, played Mercutio for a month; then they would switch roles. As I was technically out of work and hard up, and also as I had seen and much admired John I had decided to save up for this switch. I wrote and tore up letters to Larry. I hardly knew what to say: but ended by trying to point out that had I had any idea who he was I would hardly have been so gratuitously rude, but would, in any case, have made the same answer stating my position: all very feeble but the best I could do.

I was staggered by the result, which was a letter by return saying he had been startled, too, for the moment, but after all I was only saying out loud what all London was saying behind his back. In any case he considered it my duty to see him attempting both roles and he included four stalls – seats I could never have afforded. Well, his Romeo was splendid, although some critics were saying that with all his dynamism he could not quite manage the verse. But his Mercutio was electrifying. My afternoon was not so misspent: I had met Laurence Olivier.

★ George Devine (1910–66), a founder director of the English Stage Company (at the Royal Court from 1956). Originally an actor. He was married to one of the Motleys, Sophie Harris.

The next meeting must have been some two years later. I had taken, in a very amateurish way, to photography in theatres, telling the various companies' press agents that I had been commissioned by *The Sketch* to photograph their plays – of course I hadn't, but as *The Sketch* would often publish my pictures I was never caught out. This didn't work at the Old Vic, so when the 1936–7 season with Larry started I virtually forced my way on to the stage there and, remembering me, he was very charming and let me snatch a few shots each time. My early pictures of all those great parts are now the only visible record of those wonderful early performances of Henry V, Coriolanus, as Toby Belch in *Twelfth Night* for which I think he wore his first false nose: there is a legend that when he was first interviewed by Elsie Fogerty at the Central School she said, "Yes, a splendid actor's face", then a pause and laying her finger on his nose at the bridge she said "A weakness here – you will always have a little difficulty with that." Whether it is true or false, he would always resort to nosepaste when he could and became very good with it – indeed he became a master of make-up in general and I think Sir Toby must have been his first nose job. The picture in my cutting book shows it well, very effective but rather coarse.

By the time I photographed his Macbeth, it had become very fine. Indeed that whole make-up was wonderful: I remember taking the pictures into his dressing room – I never published unpassed photographs – and although it was December, and I don't suppose the Vic was over heated, he had stripped off the enormously heavy Motley clothes. I remember the banquet robes were made of blue flooding felt and weighed a ton: I had announced myself through the closed door and got a "Come in Angus," and there he stood, that great shaggy lion's head exaggerating the slender white boy's body while his dresser sprayed him with cologne.

Then in the next season was his Iago to Ralph Richardson's Othello, about which there is another legend:

Larry: I wonder what motivated Iago to have risen to that position, he must have been an intelligent man.

Tony Guthrie (directing): I've always wondered, it's one of the difficulties of the play.

Larry: I know Tony, let's play it with Iago in love with Othello.

Guthrie: What a wonderful idea – but we must never let Ralphie know!

But it was that first Hamlet, certainly my first and I think also Larry's Baylis that I remember best. I had taken two long shots and then pushed Larry under a stage floodlight and exposed two plates when a strident voice was heard "Who is this holding up our rehearsal?" "It's Mr McBean, Miss Baylis, taking pictures for *The Sketch.*" "*The Sketch!* We don't want that kind of person here." And, please remember, that it was not the newspaper, but the rather grand society glossy magazine!

I suppose one of those two plates is the best picture I have ever taken and one of the very few photographs which hang on my wall. The make-up is minimal – no nose paste but two strange tricks: the thickness of his eyelids back to his eyes is painted white, increasing their intensity – an old ballet trick – and a strange line is drawn lightly from the inner corner of his eyes diagonally across his face. I commented on this and he told me he had learned to do it in Hollywood – "tired boy stuff," he said. "I don't suppose it shows much to the audience, but it's good for photography." Also I think that he had widened his forehead with a bit of shading, but I could be mistaken.

It was taken so long ago that I think that I can look at it now quite objectively and realise that it is a very good portrait indeed, but then I have possibly never phtographed a better performance, certainly not of *Hamlet*, and I have learned that is impossible to make a good picture of a ham performance. You would have to be a very dud photographer to take a bad picture of that one.

I had caught the attention of Vivien Leigh even earlier, and so early in their careers I had the very great fortune to be one of the accredited – indeed the official photographer – to the accepted "Royals" of the British stage. Excepting the war years, I took photographs of virtually everything they did in this country. Of course they must have liked my work, but I think it was as much to do with my rule never to show my shots even to the companies who had commissioned them until they had been seen and approved by the stars.

It would be tedious to list all the shows I photographed or the visits made to my studio, but they were extraordinarily faithful, if I can use the term. Larry even insisted, against the inclination of the tobacco company, to use me to do the publicity pictures for the short-lived "Olivier" cigarette scheme, and my silhouette picture of him with a drift of smoke was even on the packet. I could never understand why he did that job. I suppose the monetary inducement was too great to refuse: it was always said that he did his films, wonderful though they were, just to finance his theatre work, which was quite often in the non-commercial theatre, the Old Vic, the National, Stratford and even Chichester, all of which I photographed. This could not have been very financially rewarding, important though it was in the history of the British Theatre.

There are a couple of things I must record about the 1955 Stratford-upon-Avon season. One was his make-up as Titus Andronicus. He was young to be playing the part, and his makeup for performances must have been quite elaborate – to tell from the stage. However for the photo call he put on the most elaborate and subtle face, which must have taken hours. As I have said before, he was a master of make-up and the photographs show the face of an elderly man – still vital and healthy, finely seamed and puckered as faces go when exposed to too much sun and wind. It photographed remarkably well without any softening of my customary harsh lighting and focus.

The other thing I remember had nothing to do with photography, although I was able to catch it in a shot: that was the remarkable moment when he threw himself from a ten-foot high rostrum in *Coriolanus* to be caught almost at floor level by a group of – I'm sure – quite terrified young actors. I watched him rehearse it again and again one morning, and well remember the great gasp that came up from the audience the first night. For a long period he went right out to Notting Hill Gate to a gymnasium for a workout with an athlete's coach – I wonder how many actors keep themselves in that kind of athletic training?

But now things were getting difficult for me in the theatre. The two-and-a-half hours of stage time I required to get my pictorial effects were being found more and more difficult to afford. I found myself having to share the time for the official photo call with ever more photographers and finally, by the tme of Larry's great Othello, I was able to squeeze in only about twenty minutes on the stage, and this by waiting hours into the night. I could only catch a bit of the death of Desdemona and a few good heads of Larry in that quite remarkable make-up, so the play, important as it was, was never properly recorded at all. This was 1964, the year of my sixtieth birthday, and dear Larry found time to open the Kodak Exhibition of all my Shakespeare pictures. He arrived early from a day-long rehearsal of *Othello*, even before I had had time to go round the exhibition myself – I had left the selection and arrangement entirely to Kodak and had no idea what they had chosen to hang. Larry asked me to show him round the large showroom and we passed picture after picture – no Olivier – I was in despair with worry when we went round the last corner and there from floor to ceiling, at least ten feet high, was a great head of Othello – almost overwhelming – and also at the side a screen of smaller pictures of practically all his Shakespeare roles.

The speech he made introducing the show was warm and very amusing. He said that we had been married for thirty years "strictly in camera", and ended by presenting me with a great cake in the form of a camera. One paper, reporting the event, said the cake was surrounded by sixty flash bulbs which went off as I took it . . . alas, not true . . . but a story so amusing that I have told it so often that it has almost become so. It was just a cake, and as I found later, quite inedible!

However, sadly, after this flourish, things gradually got worse and I found myself not only sharing the official call with the whole of the press and having to take the pictures with existing stage lighting, quite unsuited to any photography, especially to mine. And then, in the next year, 1965, came – for me – the end.

Larry was directing Arthur Miller's play, *The Crucible*, and we had come to the dramatic last act. Larry said that there was a moment he especially wanted on film. We stood side by side in the auditorium and he said he would flick his fingers at the precise moment: I was perforce using my small camera, hand held, and we waited and waited while the light on the stage got lower and lower and the action more and more violent. I knew it was quite impossible, for film in 1965 was not of modern speeds, but when the fingers clicked I pressed the button and the camera didn't register – it had agreed with me – quite impossible, and in any case it was out of film. Larry looked at me and I looked back, packed up my camera and left the Vic for the last time thinking that was the end of my long friendship with Larry – however I was wrong.

A while later my secretary told me: "Sir Laurence Olivier on the phone wants to speak to you." He was rehearsing *The Dance of Death* and he asked me if I could possibly take all my equipment to the rehearsal rooms and take a "Period Wedding Picture". He would explain when I got there. The finished picture was needed for filming the next day and only I could possibly take it.

So I went off deeply intrigued, to find that I had to produce a picture of Larry and Geraldine McEwan being married thirty years earlier. "And even you and your retouching can't make us look twenty," said Larry.

So I took a period looking shot of the two youngsters in the cast, the boy in uniform and the girl in an Edwardian wedding dress, then went home and after a long search found a suitable picture taken of Larry forty years earlier at home in that house in Cheyne Walk with the copper door, and one of Geraldine taken in a play twenty or so years later. I printed them and stuck them onto the picture of the young people, copied it and tottered off to bed at about two in the morning, only to be woken up at 9.30 to be told that Larry had forgotten to tell me that he was wearing a white order across his chest, and as it was mentioned in the script it must be there . . . and that the picture was wanted by lunch time!

Since writing the above I was looking through my studio visitors book for a reference and I came upon an entry, for 9.10.61:

Your rice puddings are excellent

L. Olivier

– a take off, of course, of almost any entry into the visitors books of almost every theatrical digs' landladies.

MARK AMORY

MARK AMORY

Educated at Eton and Christ Church, Oxford, Mark Amory has been publisher, journalist, biographer (*Lord Dunsany*, 1972), theatre critic and is now Literary Editor of the *Spectator*. He has edited the letters of Evelyn Waugh and Ann Fleming. As well as the experience he describes here, he was ghost for the Kabaka of Uganda.

THE AUTHOR

"Of course Larry's a gangster," remarked a formidable actress, "that's why he was so good as Macbeth." With no other personal information I was apprehensive when first meeting Lord Olivier with whom I was to work on his autobiography in 1980. I got off to a poor start by failing to recognise him. The man who came through the right door at the correct time was too short for Henry V, too urbane for Archie Rice, too ordinary for Richard III. His cheeks are pink and his face remarkably unlined, which has allowed him to go on playing much younger than his age even on film in merciless close-up. His white hair can be dyed, as can his moustache, which is after all expendable though without it his lips, as he points out, are thin and cruel. When he began to grow his beard that was white too and the first sign that he was going to say yes to Lear on television. People say that he looks like a businessman but is that perhaps because they met him on some committee where a businessman was required? He seemed more elusive, with a lighter touch in his London house, a conscientious host, a fond father, hard to add much to that, impossible to guess what he thought of *me*.

Polite and considerate, he took me aback during the next few weeks by calling me darling; it was not till he varied this with "Kurt" (a friend of his daughters) that it dawned on me that he simply could not remember my name.

We set to work. My plan was to make many hours of tape-recordings, fifty-seven as it turned out, before trying to produce something coherent on paper. He darted from subject to subject, decade to decade, hoping to elude anything so mundane, so expected, as chronological order. Unimpressed when I exhibited some piece of arcane knowledge, he was uncritical, as far as I could tell, of ignorance, when, for example, I entirely forgot that he had played Antony – though he did say "Yes, I made quite a success with him." Above all, he was professional, though in an unfamiliar profession. If he found retelling familiar stories tedious, he gave no sign. Only once in the fifty-seven hours did he gesture for the machine to be turned off; I leaned forward, eager for some private revelation and must admit to being disappointed when it was the name of an actor whom he thought less than perfect at assuming authentic accents. He had himself just played General MacArthur in the film *Inchon* (which seems destined never to be seen for legal and financial reasons), had taken immense pains to track down old recordings and said that the fascinating thing was that they were inconsistent – various influences slid and sidled across his vowel sounds. Olivier was pleased with the result and with the recital of the Lord's Prayer at the end of the film, the challenge of making fresh some of the most familiar words in the language without seeming tricky. That was, I think, cut, but the whole performance may be lost.

His memory is not as it was, but then it was extraordinary. On the last night of a Stratford season he recited the names of everybody connected with the company – the number ninety-nine sticks in my less precise mind – when clearly to miss even one would be appalling and there was no progress or even grammar to act as a reminder. Now he remembers his childhood better than this morning, as is normal in the old, but he remembers the theatre just as vividly and occasionally, very occasionally, bang wrong. He enjoyed running through the cast of productions he was in fifty or sixty years ago and was annoyed if he got stuck. Suggestions from me that a name could be looked up later, by which I meant that it did not actually matter, were brushed aside; he wanted to remember *now*. He also did something which often happens in plays but not in life: when telling a story he recreated the mood. Talking of unhappy years with a former wife, most people would be deliberately detached, perhaps even humorous – he seemed to relive the moment. Recalling a stormy board meeting at the National he crashed his fist down on the table and fixed me with such a glare that I could not meet his eyes. More happily, when

Shakespeare and in particular *Hamlet* came up – and he would vault over a dozen topics to bring him in – he liked to quote passages and as he did so his arm would rise in a gesture, his back straighten, his chin point, his eyes flash and the years drop from him in a way that was astonishing and moving. One of my few adroit moments as a host was when he came to lunch at the beginning of the Falklands War. "It's just like that bit in *Hamlet*," I said, "How does it go? A little patch of ground that hath no profit . . ." and we were into "How all occasions do inform against me" in a flash. A more nervous moment came when Teresa Waugh asked him which were his favourite novels and he replied *Pride and Prejudice*, *Wuthering Heights* and Arnold Bennett's best, we couldn't think of the title, he got it, *The Old Wives' Tale*. After a moment's pause he said he had been in films of two of them and Teresa said yes she had noticed that. Another momentary pause and he added, "There was no part for me in *The Old Wives' Tale*," and laughed. He can, however, be severe. Lightly, as when a silly girl bubbled on about how difficult it was for her to get herself taken seriously just because she was a blonde; with a pointed glance at her parting he replied, "But my dear, it was your decision." Or frighteningly, though even then with charm, as when he was telephoned in the country at two o'clock on a Sunday. Picking up the receiver he immediately launched into a furious oration which began "I did think there was one hour of the week when an Englishman was safe from intrusion . . ." going on for some time and ending with a sudden change of tone, "Who is it? Ah, dear boy, how nice to hear your voice. Joan will be with you in a moment."

Sometimes we met in London; more fruitfully I would go to his cottage near Brighton up a dreadful track that was supposed to choke off visitors. I only half-believed him when he said that he swam fifty lengths before breakfast but soon found that it was true and that twenty was enough for me. Sometimes we were looked after by a couple, sometimes the family was there, sometimes we were alone. Then he cooked my breakfast and enjoyed showing bits of knowledge that might be unexpected – that it is best to start boiling an egg in cold water, for instance. He was less well when we started than when we finished and had a thorough understanding of all the different coloured pills he took: "I may be a bit deaf today. I have to take two of these because the cramp is painful." At one stage he was fond of an electric blue, fake satin jacket that he had been given at the end of filming *The Jazz Singer* with Neil Diamond. It said "Diamond" on the back and "The Baron" on the lapel. Another time he wore socks on his hands because they were cold; this did not prevent him from telephoning. Talking with the gardener and the garden itself gave pleasure; typically he knew the Latin names of the shrubs and enjoyed saying them. Also typically he is able to remark "I know a bank where wild thyme grows . . . it's just round that corner, as a matter of fact," because he has planted one with all the flowers Shakespeare names.

I should have been suspicious when he took his typewriter with him to stay with the Waltons* in Capri. Not that there was anything that I could have done about it or even wanted to. He came back determined to write the whole book himself and duly did so. I hovered around, suggested that some bits were obscure or in the wrong place or that some adjectives might come out. I recorded one exchange:

L.O. (reading): . . . and peeped open the door.
Me: Um, I think you could say "peeped *through* the door".
L.O.: Well it was up all these stairs, and the Albert Hall is so vast, when I looked down I thought "Goodness what a huge . . ." etc.
Me: Well perhaps "pushed open".
L.O.: I like peeped open.
Me: Or "peeped through the open . . ."
L.O.: It seems to me all right as it is.
Me: Well, it doesn't er, really, quite make sense.
L.O. (still genial): It makes sense to me.

The only unusual thing about this exchange was that I prevailed in the end. Of course a real autobiography is more interesting than a ghosted one. Olivier's seems to me however more frank than revealing. I have assumed here that he is a great actor about whom it is worth recording trivia. What an autobiography might have revealed is either "How does he do it?" or "What sort of man is he?" His answer to both these questions is basically "I don't know". And this may be his secret. The most versatile of great

* William Walton (1902–83). One of the greatest twentieth-century English composers. Wrote the music for Olivier's *Henry V*, *Hamlet* and *Richard III*. Knighted 1951. With his wife Susana lived in Capri.

actors – there are parts that are not naturally his, like Richard II or Falstaff, but it would be a bold man who said definitively that he could never have made a success of them – he pours his talents into a part and it seems to fit. He has no *persona*. He has never been accused of simply playing himself as no one is quite sure what that would be. Archie Rice may have used bits of autobiography but it was very much a performance; his playing of little men, Berenger in Ionesco's *Rhinoceros* for instance, give no impression of being the "real" man (indeed they seem to me the only category in which he fails – he does not agree). By being nobody he can become anybody and then – and this is his genius – thrilling to watch as well.

MELVYN
BRAGG

MELVYN BRAGG

Melvyn Bragg (b. 1939) author of twelve novels, including *The Hired Man* (1969), *Josh Lawton* (1972) and *The Maid of Buttermere* (1987), has been the Presenter and Editor of *The South Bank Show* for Independent Television since 1978. He is Head of Arts for London Weekend Television and Deputy Chairman of Border Television. His book *Laurence Olivier* was published subsequent to a lengthy television interview conducted in 1982.

ECCLESIASTICAL ECHOES

"And I suppose I'll end up in Westminster Abbey."

Westminster Abbey. Olivier's sense of his own destiny might seem from the outside to be a little over-vaunting. That suggestion would ruffle him. He likes and cleaves to the appearance of the old crypto-caricature of the Englishman – stiff lipped and frugal of speech under fire: but Westminster Abbey will be his earthly destination, so why pretend? And, that reference to the Abbey came at the beginning of a statement in which he sent himself up as an actor and as a *Lord* – Baron Olivier of Brighton. Perhaps the "Westminster Abbey" was "Just for Fun" – the slogan he suggested accompany his new coat of arms. Yet his own sense of Englishness and others sense of his Englishness could be seen as one of the shaping elements in his work. A rich, varied, poetic, anciently rooted Englishness which loves to conceal itself inside a peaceful, composed exterior: very like Westminster Abbey.

Englishness both nourished him and is cherished by him. His public school – St Edward's, Oxford – was in the Anglican ecclesiastical tradition, perpetuating the strong C. of E. strand in his early life. Other archetypal Englishmen at St Edward's at that time included Douglas Bader and Kenneth Grahame. Olivier went through that traditional "artist-type" sensitive schoolboy ritual of being unpopular, disliked, the outsider, a loner. In True Brit, Boy's Own style, though, Olivier not only saved up his suffering for later revenges, he hit back, outrageously. He played Puck in the school's production of the *Dream*, fighting and flirting across the old school hall like an unbottled demon, misting the minds of the hearties who thenceforward offered him their arm for a stroll at break times.

English, too, in the love of Dickensian jumble and the lovingly entertained setbacks and humiliations of his early struggles in Clacton (minor role in *The Barber and the Cow*) and all points north, the walk-ons, the landladies, the gaffes; in his consistent returns to Shakespeare; in the letter to *The Times* complaining about the removal of kippers from the menu on the London to Brighton train; in the knowledgeable love of gardening; in his practical jokes – disguising himself and joining a group of tourists touring Chichester, when he was director, and making himself very unpopular with them by complaining about the waste of money it all represented; cricket, of course; and so on onto the club ties, antique politeness, anti-intellectualism, sudden aloofness.

Yet does "English" fit the long and recurrent drive to form his own companies and totally control the show – to be managing director, director, dramaturge, leading man, company owner . . . and at the same time to star in American movies, keep a close watch on his peers, live the life of Riley, be a Baron indeed of all the territories at his command? And the stories of ferocity, the rumours of theatrical wars, the endless playing with character, his own, the author's, the audience's? The well-cut, bespoke English Disguise carries us only so far even though it does point him towards Westminster Abbey.

*　　*　　*

In all the time we were filming with Olivier – which straddled over half a year – in his house, in theatres, with his friends, watching his own performances on film, strolling along the front in Brighton, seated like a Sultan receiving guests at a party in Chelsea – he was most moved, least ambiguous, most passionate, in a church. All Saints', Margaret Street, middle of London, difficult to park there now, easy to miss.

His mother managed to winkle him into the Choir School when he was nine. His elder brother, Dickie, was already there. The choir numbered fourteen and they boarded. It was High Anglican – "Oh, *very* High," he said, leaning on the *H* with emphasis and delicacy – "incense, my dear" – and he'll mock what he loves

with a fleeting caricature of genteel camp. But not that afternoon.

We had been to Overton's for lunch. "That's what I call civilised
– you ask for half a dozen oysters and they give you seven." "And
just a little champagne?" "Well, a glass, or two, oh, if you insist
– and what about the sole?" For a man come through six years of
ravaging precipitous illnesses, he flourishes in enjoying himself.
"Just a little bitsie more of the champers I think, don't you?" And
two puddings: a pudding and then strawberry ice cream "with just
a trickle, just the veriest littlest drop of this loverly bubbly; yes –
of course you will."

The driver circled the block with the usual central London
desperation, looking for a parking place, urged on by Olivier, on
the scent, in the hunt, "Over there! No – too small. Turn right
here. *There!* No, dammit madam we were in front of you but bless
the ladies, how do you do she's beaten us to it – *there!*" He stopped
in the middle of the street and we walked. It was one of the only
times – if not *the* only time during the entire shoot when Olivier
walked with anything approaching his stage energy. The walk
now is measured, very: sometimes even a little faltering. He strode
into All Saints' – had not been there for "donkey's years. Don-keys
years!" – and saying "Did you check with the precentor, the vicar
would be too gránd, did you ask him if he minded an old boy
pottering around the place for half an hour – down memory lane?
The precentor would have to check with the church wardens, you
see – look!"

"Look!"

"It *is* the most beautiful church!"

"Look!"

"We came in there, you see, processed, O yes, very pious,
swinging the incense, carrying the cross – and there – you stood
there – when you became solo boy which I am happy to inform
you yours truly damn well managed to be and just look at the
ceiling, perfect acoustics – singing here every day, you see, my
darling, darling mother came to hear us and a bit of Society
sometimes, the best choir in London we were, not the biggest but
the *best*, everyone said so, they came to hear us, and it's here we
started with the plays – I followed Dickie in that as in everything
– but it was the singing really, the psalms, the ritual, this is where
it all started, O yes. Not just for me, I'm sure, for all of us, boys,
then, whatever we might do – dedication, the – awfully sentimental

isn't it? – but true, *service*, doing it for the Greater Glory – O yes – no question, *none*: this is where it started."

He was crying by then: ignoring the tears, forcing you to ignore them too. "I *loved* the singing."

★   ★   ★

Of his first wife, Jill Esmond (or "My very first wife," as he says) he speaks most affectionately; of his second wife, Vivien Leigh, he speaks in torment; of Joan Plowright, his third and present wife, he speaks with perpetual adoration.

It is hard enough to learn the truth or even half the truth about anyone's private life: God knows what Olivier is like, in love, in private, in a marriage; what happens to the masks and disguises, whether they multiply, whether they are exchanged for other masks, whether they fall off to reveal the tooth and claw of tiredness, anger, loneliness, who knows?

What is clear is that he wants no attention directed from Joan Plowright. She has seen and helped him switch course decisively in his career, in the mid–fifties, shared the making of Chichester with him and then the haul of the National Theatre, bringing up a family and developing her own considerable career the while: she has seen him through the illnesses, guided him to television where his roles in *The Collection, Cat on a Hot Tin Roof, Brideshead* and *Voyage Around My Father* more than compensated for flaked enamel parts in some of the late films. Now she watches him in their ample cottage in Sussex and in the London house, as he tacks and weaves his way back to strength, family, now and then, reaching for the phone for the doctor, needing the full battery of pills, but still inimitably There. "Joanie," "My Joanie; she's very clever you know: I always listened to her." And she, of him, "When he came to the Court (to do *The Entertainer*) of course we all thought that you couldn't act if you didn't wear jeans and a lot of us were suspicious of Sir Laurence, all that grandeur, we regarded ourselves, in a way, as opposed to all that he represented. Well that feeling lasted until he got into the first rehearsal and then it vanished. You can't be on a stage with him and not know, well, how marvellous he is." Does he compete? "Only if somebody tries to outshine him. There are those who try, have tried, you know. None of them can do it." Who was it who said that being on stage with him was like being in a cage full of lions?

We went to Chichester with both of them. Olivier spent his time talking about that hair-raising first season which just made it by the blessing of *Uncle Vanya*, praising Tynan and retrospectively most staunchly justifying his own good sense in hiring him for the National. ("It was Joanie who persuaded me, you know: when he wrote, asking, I was all for getting back at him because of the nasty things he'd written about poor Vivien – but Joanie said, no, think about it, you need him; and she was right as usual;") and the rest of the time including Joan in every second breath he took or observation he made. They posed in the car park for photographers. Joan with that tentative, apprehensive sense of reluctance, Olivier with the playfulness, the flitting and flirting manner; arm in arm. The photos came out very well.

★   ★   ★

The first occasion on which I spent some time in his private company was when I laid on a dinner for William Walton at the Garrick Club. When the man in the over-large pin-striped suit trudged into the room I had no idea who he was. The spectacles were City-Clerkish Heavy; the clothes correct but a little crumpled; the air deeply diffident; in all a brilliant disguise for one of the most famous faces and forces in the theatre this century. Laurence Olivier, the retired old gentleman, well dug into his shell, only wispily, only accidentally, it seemed, taking the odd peck at the outside world. He's very old, we all thought, very frail: the terrible series of illnesses, almost died several times, you know, miracle he's here at all, does those film cameos because it's all his strength can manage, you know, and the money. Those days at the National did not bring in much money, a young family, wants to provide for them, the voice, that voice, so thin now, get him a chair.

And some of it is true – the battering illnesses, the frightening cures, the whole body in disorder: but he was only waiting. Walton and his wife held the table and Olivier smiled, returned a compliment, corroborated a story, ate and drank carefully, so slight we all thought – remember Othello! remember Heathcliff! Remember . . . and dead eyes, no acting now for Archie Rice: dead eyes, someone who had come through but to what? Compared with the glories of his years of health and fame and almost unimaginable vigour – for what?

But like a lizard on a rock, he was only waiting for the moment to start. After all, it was a stage of sorts, this dinner table, this room. He was surrounded by paintings of the great theatrical dead. The Club itself carried the name of one of the most celebrated actors in history. There were candles, some faces new to him, the coffee was on the table; it was somehow plain that, unjust as it was for us to impose, we were waiting for Olivier to make his entrance.

And as in a fairy tale, the little old gentleman in the dandruff-flecked, over-large pin-stripe, came on, released a cluster of fire-works – anecdotes, brilliantly exact mimicry, coy seeming self-satires, cannonades of belly-laughter stories – and then said it was time for him to go home. He had a long way to travel – into Sussex, the cottage, he lived there most of the time now, so nice to see you all, again the frayed Anglican air; polite, old fashioned, a church warden no doubt, a man who had always caught the 8.22. Perfect camouflage, conserving his energy with an extraordinary sense of its capacity.

"I owe you a thank you very much," the driver said, the next time we met. "On account of you gave me Sir Laurence Olivier to drive back. He slept most of the way. Then, when we got there – makes me a cup of tea with his own hands. Three o'clock in the morning and he's going like the clappers. He's got to be a great man." So on top of all that carefulness, a sudden generous profligacy. By then, we had already asked him if we could make a film biography on him to coincide with the publication of his memoirs. "I always wanted," he said "to be unrecognisable from one part to the next."

JOHN MORTIMER

JOHN MORTIMER

By profession a barrister, John Mortimer (b. 1923) is best known as the author of such plays as *Dock Brief* (1957), *A Voyage Round My Father* (1970), in which Olivier played in the 1982 television version, and for the creation of the television series, *Rumpole of the Bailey*. He was the adaptor of Waugh's *Brideshead Revisited* for television and in 1984 wrote the script of *The Ebony Tower* by John Fowles. His own bestselling novel, *Paradise Postponed*, was serialised on television in 1986. He was awarded the CBE in 1986.

THAT
STRAIN AGAIN!
IT HAD A
DYING FALL

The house was invaded, converted to a film set. A false wall in the sitting room imprisoned my books. Electric cables snaked up the stairs and huge lights glared at the cracks in the plaster. Out in the garden an outcrop of plastic cups testified to the length of the eighty strong film unit's stay. In the kitchen my family held their breaths or set out for the kettle on tip-toe. Upstairs Laurence Olivier was playing my father's death scene in the bed in which I had watched my father's life end. "I'm always angry when I'm dying," he said my father's almost last words, an actor playing a man who had had the courage to treat death as a sort of performance. At last the scene was over and we could all breathe, relax, talk again, go out into the garden to get tea and slabs of cake from the butty wagon. Laurence Olivier came down the stairs beaming, rejuvenated, as he always seems to be, by playing any death scene. "What an impossible character your father must have been," he said. "Of course, it's absolutely vital not to try and play him for sympathy." I was happy then, knowing that if Olivier wasn't playing for sympathy, everyone who saw him would sympathise immediately with the central character in *A Voyage Round My Father*, just as he made the audience adore Richard III. All the same, it's hard to write dispassionately of an actor who has been your father, and died in your father's bed.

A lifetime before that, when I was fourteen years old, I sat beside my father in the Old Vic and saw *Hamlet* in what used to be known, as though it were in some way an unusual experience, as its "entirety". I can remember everything about that production, the shape of the set, the taste of the coffee and sandwiches in the long interval, and Olivier's surprising way with the verse which, as was his wont, my father was intoning audibly from the front row of the stalls. He was a young, intensely physical and constantly dangerous Hamlet. The next year we saw Coriolanus die in an extraordinary and athletic manner, rolling down a long flight of steps almost into our laps. Very young but not in the least athletic or dangerous, I had no idea that so many years later I would write three old men's parts for him in two of which he would die unathletically and in bed.

There was this old actor, on the stage playing Macbeth, and his company manager had to tell him that a fellow from the electricity board had come to cut off the lights. So he snatches up a hat and cloak, dashes up to Macbeth and says, conspiratorially, "My Lord, there is one without who threatens, but for the passage of certain gold between ye, to douse your glim!" Laurence Olivier loves this story, which might have been handed down from the old days in the Lyceum and retold by actors in the bars of Brighton and on the platform at Crewe during a Sunday change over. He also relishes the legend of Kean who, when someone in the pit called out, "You're drunk!" during *Richard III*, staggered down to the footlights and slurred out, "You think *I'm* drunk? Wait till you see the Duke of Buckingham." His laughter is pitched quite high, his cheeks become pink and his eyes moist with delight, but you would be mistaken to believe that under all this "old love" chat and the theatrical chestnuts there is not an immensely serious and startlingly original artist at work. Scratch an actor, Olivier has said, and you find an actor. In his case if you scratch an old actor laddy you are likely to find a genius.

Undoubtedly the greatest theatrical season in my lifetime was the Olivier, Richardson and Guthrie regime at the New Theatre with the Old Vic Company. There he created his Richard III with a voice which used three notes in a parody of memories of Irving and a character founded on a peculiarly loathsome Austro–New York producer he had suffered under. And there, in a dazzling display of technical virtuosity, he played Oedipus, and Mr Puff in *The Critic* as a double bill. King Oedipus, condemned by the gods for a crime he didn't know he'd committed, uttered, at the terrible moment of his blinding, a scream which has echoed in horror in my memory ever since.

"Tell me about the scream in *Oedipus*," I asked Olivier, still remembering it at the end of the 1970s when we had dinner in a small hotel, The Worsley Arms, in Yorkshire, near to Castle Howard and the shooting of *Brideshead Revisited*. The darkly handsome, doomed Greek king had given way to Lord Marchmain, returning home to die in an ornate Chinese bed having delighted himself, and his future audiences, with a series of mischievous and teasing attacks on his immediate family. Olivier himself wore the scars of his heroic war with an illness which would have defeated ordinary mortals. Perhaps it was this campaign which gave him the upright and brave appearance of a retired military man, dressed in country tweeds. We consumed a large quantity of white burgundy and claret and he told me exactly how he had come by Oedipus's scream.

"First of all I thought of foxes. Little foxes with their paws caught in a steel trap," he held out thin wrists, stiff and helpless, "and then I heard about how they catch ermine. It was a great help to me when I heard about that. You don't know how they catch ermine?" He looked at me in simulated wonder, astonished at my ignorance of facts vital to the acting business. "In the Arctic they put down salt and the ermine comes to lick it. It's caught when its tongue freezes to the ice. I thought about that when I screamed as Oedipus. It wasn't an *ah* or an *ugh* scream. More of an *err*."

So for a terrible moment, with the make-up blood streaming down his cheeks, Olivier became a small, desperate animal with its soft, warm tongue frozen to the ice, for reasons it could no more understand than could the tortured Oedipus.

★   ★   ★

The sixties were happy times at the National Theatre, when the offices were in a series of leaking pre-fabs and the Old Vic was as exciting as when I had coffee and sandwiches there during the long interval with my father. Olivier gave the place an extraordinary glamour. He had led his troops into battle as Henry V, and smouldered with irreconcilable rage as Heathcliff, and now he stalked the pre-fabs in a business suit improbably disguised as an executive producer accompanied by his éminence grise, the élitist Brechtian and immaculate left-wing hedonist, the late Ken Tynan.

I had translated a Feydeau farce, *Puce à l'Oreille*, which we called *Flea in her Ear*, and we sat in one of the pre-fabs, occasionally refreshed with apples and champagne, reading the English version aloud with Albert Finney, who was to play in it. Olivier discussed the placing of each joke, the shape of every sentence. He had learned, he always said, so much from the timing of great comic performers like Jack Benny and Bob Hope and such lessons were not only useful in comedy. George Robey's diction helped him to put across the great tragic arias with stunning clarity, and a version of the double-take was important to his tragic roles. He remembered Charlie Chaplin, who talked, it seems, somewhat portentously "in his half American, half Cockney accent; but of course he couldn't escape from the unlikely fact that he was a genius. I remember him saying, 'Hamlet was a young man who was subject to all life's *stimuli*.' Well, years later, I used the same rather pompous inflection on the word '*anthropophagi*' in Othello's speech to the senators, so Charlie Chaplin got me a nice laugh."

So moments from the great comics flicker through his Hamlet, his Macbeth and his Lear, confirming my own belief that you can't do anything seriously unless you can act, or write, comedy.

Three years ago now I wrote another part for Olivier, the cantankerous old painter Henry Breasley in an adaptation of John Fowles' short novel *The Ebony Tower*. The story concerns a somewhat over serious young abstract artist who travels to France to interview an impossible old genius who lives attended by two young girls. The serious interviewer tries to pluck the heart out of the old man's mystery. By the time I wrote my version of *The Ebony Tower* I thought I knew Olivier's dialogue and could make Henry Breasley talk like him in his most mischievous and "dear boy" moods. Breasley is a supreme artist who can't explain his own magical powers.

"Don't give a toss where the ideas come from. Never have. Just grateful for them. You know there's really no point in asking me questions . . ." and, "Just paint (or act). Leave the clever talk to the poor sods who can't."

Of course Olivier delivered the lines marvellously, with the rising inflection of a slightly querulous old man constantly startled by the immensity of his own talent. But he isn't, of course he's not, Henry Breasley. He *does* know where the ideas come from and he sets out to look for them painstakingly. He described how he is endlessly watching people, or hearing snatches of conversations, learning walks, nervous tics, plummy accents, affectations, and remembering speech rhythms. He tries the effect of putting today's street faces into other periods, or visiting the National Portrait Gallery to think about lighting and make-up. The actor, no less than the writer, has to be continually on the look out.

The criticism which used to be made of Olivier's acting was that it was so technically brilliant, so hugely daring and inventive, that it must, in some strange way, lack heart. These ideas, fashionable in the days of so-called "method acting", arise from a plodding distrust of brilliance in the arts; anything really clever, it's thought, must be in some way insincere. That is, of course, rubbish. No two artists were ever so technically assured as Shakespeare and Mozart. Olivier's great effects may come from a brilliant technique and a careful collection of observations, memories of comics, old actors and people on trains, but they remain unforgettable. Three in particular will live with me always, Oedipus's scream of agony, the moment when the grief of Archie Rice, the Entertainer, bursts out in the voice of an old, fat negress singing the blues, and a speech in *A Voyage Round My Father* when my father's helpless laughter at one of his oldest and best legal anecdotes slithered into the choking gasp of his approaching death. Such moments may be sought for and found by the use of many superb technical devices but they become extraordinary revelations of the splendours and miseries of our life on earth.

KEY TO THE FRONTISPIECE
by Antony Sher

1 – Mr Puff (*The Critic*). 2 – Henry V. 3 – Hamlet. 4 – Lear.
5 – Macbeth. 6 – James Tyrone (*Long Day's Journey Into Night*).
7 – Lord Olivier (on being introduced into the House of Lords).
8 – Othello. 9 – Archie Rice (*The Entertainer*). 10 – Richard III.
11 – Maxim de Winter (*Rebecca*). 12 – Oedipus. 13 – Romeo.
14 – Edgar (*The Dance of Death*). 15 – Shylock. 16 – Clifford
Mortimer (*Voyage Round My Father*). 17 – Hotspur (*Henry IV,
Part I*). 18 – Dr Szell (*Marathon Man*). 19 – Coriolanus.

CHRONOLOGY

OLIVIER

Chronological Table of Parts and Productions

1924

	St Christopher's School, Letchworth	*Macbeth*	Lennox
Nov	Century	*Byron*	Suliot Officer

1925

Feb	Regent (Fellowship of Players)	*Henry IV Part 2*	Master Snare, Thomas of Clarence
Autumn	Hippodrome, Brighton and Tour	*Unfailing Instinct*	Armand St Cyr
	Hippodrome, Brighton and Tour	*The Ghost Train*	Walk-on
Autumn	Century and Tour in London	*The Tempest*	Antonio
	Century and Tour in London	*Julius Caesar*	Flavius
Dec	Empire	*Henry VIII*	Walk-on

1926

Mar	Empire	*The Cenci*	Servant to Orsino
Apr	Kingsway	*The Marvellous History of Saint Bernard*	Minstrel
Dec	Birmingham Repertory	*The Farmer's Wife*	Richard Coaker

1927

Jan	Birmingham Repertory	*Something to Talk About*	Guy Sydney
Jan	Birmingham Repertory	*The Well of the Saints*	Mat Simon
Feb	Birmingham Repertory	*The Third Finger*	Tom Hardcastle
Feb	Birmingham Repertory	*The Mannoch Family*	Peter Mannoch
Mar	Birmingham Repertory	*The Comedian*	Walk-on
Apr	Birmingham Repertory	*Uncle Vanya*	Vanya
Apr	Birmingham Repertory	*All's Well That Ends Well*	Parolles
Apr	Birmingham Repertory	*The Pleasure Garden*	Young Man
May	Birmingham Repertory	*She Stoops to Conquer*	Tony Lumpkin
June	Birmingham Repertory	*Quality Street*	Ensign Blades
Sept	Birmingham Repertory	*Bird in Hand*	Gerald Arnwood
Sept	Birmingham Repertory	*Advertising April*	Mervyn Jones
Oct	Birmingham Repertory	*The Silver Box*	Jack Barthwick
Oct	Birmingham Repertory	*The Adding Machine*	Young Man
Nov	Birmingham Repertory	*Aren't Women Wonderful!*	Ben Hawley
Dec	Birmingham Repertory	*The Road to Ruin*	Mr Milford

1928

Jan	Royal Court	*The Adding Machine*	Young Man
Jan	Royal Court	*Macbeth*	Malcolm
Mar	Royal Court	*Back to Methusaleh*	Martellus
Apr	Royal Court	*Harold*	Harold
Apr	Royal Court	*Taming of the Shrew*	A Lord
June	Royalty	*Bird in Hand*	Gerald Arnwood
Nov	Royalty	*The Dark Path*	Graham Birley
Dec	Apollo (Stage Society)	*Journey's End*	Captain Stanhope

214

1929

Jan	His Majesty's	*Beau Geste*	Michael (Beau) Geste
Mar	New	*The Circle of Chalk*	Prince Po
Apr	Lyric	*Paris Bound*	Richard Parish
June	Garrick	*The Stranger Within*	John Hardy
Sept	Eltinge, New York	*Murder on the Second Floor*	Hugh Bromilow
Dec	Fortune	*The Last Enemy*	Jerry Warrender

1930

	Film	*The Temporary Widow*	Peter Billie
	Film	*Too Many Crooks*	The Man
Mar	Arts, WC2	*After All*	Ralph
Sept	Phoenix	*Private Lives*	Victor Prynne

1931

	Film	*Potiphar's Wife (Her Strange Desire)*	Straker
	Film	*Friends and Lovers*	Lt Nichols
	Film	*The Yellow Passport (The Yellow Ticket)*	Julian Rolphe
Jan	Times Square, New York	*Private Lives*	Victor Prynne

1932

	Film	*Westward Passage*	Nick Allen

1933

	Film	*Perfect Understanding*	Nicholas Randall
	Film	*No Funny Business (The Professional Co-respondents)*	Clive Dering
Apr	Playhouse	*The Rats of Norway*	Steven Beringer
Oct	Cort, New York	*The Green Bay Tree*	Julian Dulcimer

1934

Apr	Globe	*Biography*	Richard Kurt
June	New	*Queen of Scots*	Bothwell
Oct	Lyric	*Theatre Royal*	Anthony Cavendish

1935

	Film	*Moscow Nights (I Stand Condemned)*	Captain Ignatoff
Mar	Shaftesbury	*Ringmaster*	Peter Hammond
May	Whitehall	*Golden Arrow*	Richard Harben, Director (and producer)
Oct	New	*Romeo and Juliet*	Romeo
Nov	New	*Romeo and Juliet*	Mercutio

1936

	Film	*Conquest of the Air*	Vincent Lunardi
May	Lyric	*Bees on the Boatdeck*	Robert Patch, Co-director (and co-producer)
May	Film	*As You Like It*	Orlando

1937

	Film	*Fire Over England*	Michael Ingolby
	Film	*Twenty-One Days*	Larry Durant
Jan	Old Vic	*Hamlet*	Hamlet
Feb	Old Vic	*Twelfth Night*	Sir Toby Belch
Apr	Old Vic	*Henry V*	Henry V
June	Elsinore Castle	*Hamlet*	Hamlet
Nov	Old Vic	*Macbeth*	Macbeth
Dec	New	*Macbeth*	Macbeth

1938

	Film	*The Divorce of Lady X*	Leslie Logan
Feb	Old Vic	*Othello*	Iago
Mar	Old Vic	*The King of Nowhere*	Vivaldi
Apr	Old Vic	*Coriolanus*	Coriolanus

1939

	Film	*Q Planes (Clouds Over Europe)*	Tony McVane
	Film	*Wuthering Heights*	Heathcliff
Apr	Ethel Barrymore, New York	*No Time for Comedy*	Gaylord Easterbrook
	Film	*Rebecca*	Maxim de Winter
	Film	*Pride and Prejudice*	Darcy
May	51st Street, New York	*Romeo and Juliet*	Romeo, and Director

1941

Film	*Lady Hamilton (That Hamilton Woman)*	Lord Nelson
Film	*49th Parallel (The Invaders)*	Johnnie, the trapper

1943

Film	*The Demi-Paradise (Adventure for Two)*	Ivan Dimitrievitch Kouznetoff

1943/4

Film	*Henry V*	Henry V, Director (and producer)

1944

Aug	New (Old Vic)	*Peer Gynt*	Button Moulder
Sept	New (Old Vic)	*Arms and the Man*	Sergius Saranoff
Sept	New (Old Vic)	*Richard III*	Gloucester

1945

Jan	New (Old Vic)	*Uncle Vanya*	Astrov

May–July Tour of *Peer Gynt, Arms and the Man, Richard III* to Antwerp, Ghent, Bruges and Paris (Comédie française)

May	Phoenix	*The Skin of our Teeth*	Director (and producer)
Sept	New (Old Vic)	*Henry IV Part 1*	Hotspur
Oct	New (Old Vic)	*Henry IV Part 2*	Shallow
Oct	New (Old Vic)	*Oedipus Rex*	Oedipus
Oct	New (Old Vic)	*The Critic*	Mr Puff

1946

May	Century, New York	Season of the above five plays	
Sept	New	*King Lear.*	King Lear, and Director

1947

	Film	*Hamlet*	Hamlet, Director (and producer)
May	Garrick	*Born Yesterday*	Director (and producer)

217

1948

	Tour of Australia and New Zealand (Old Vic)	*Richard III*	Gloucester
		The School for Scandal	Sir Peter Teazle, and Director
		The Skin of our Teeth	Mr Antrobus, and Director

1949

Jan	New (Old Vic)	*Richard III*	Gloucester
Jan	New (Old Vic)	*The School for Scandal*	Sir Peter Teazle, and Director
Jan	New (Old Vic)	*Antigone*	Chorus, and Director
Jan	New (Old Vic)	*The Proposal*	Director
Oct	Aldwych	*A Streetcar Named Desire*	Director (and producer)

1950

Jan	St James's	*Venus Observed*	Duke of Altair, Director (and producer)
Aug	St James's	*Captain Carvallo*	Director (and producer)
	Theatre Royal, Brighton and Tour	*The Damascus Blade*	Director (and producer)

1951

	Film	*The Magic Box*	PC 94
May	St James's	*Caesar and Cleopatra*	Caesar (and producer)
May	St James's	*Antony and Cleopatra*	Antony (and producer)
Dec	Ziegfeld, New York	Appeared in the above two plays	

1952

	Film	*Carrie*	George Hurstwood
Jan	St James's	*The Happy Time*	Co-producer
Feb	Century, New York	*Venus Observed*	Director
Feb	Film	*The Beggar's Opera*	Macheath (and co-producer)
Oct	St James's	*Othello*	Producer

1953

Nov	Phoenix	*The Sleeping Prince*	Grand Duke, and Director
Aug	St James's	*Anastasia*	Producer

1954

	Film	*Richard III*	Gloucester, and Director
Apr	St James's	*Waiting for Gillian*	Producer
July	Duke of York's	*Meet a Body*	Producer

1955

Apr	Memorial, Stratford	*Twelfth Night*	Malvolio
June	Memorial, Stratford	*Macbeth*	Macbeth
Aug	Memorial, Stratford	*Titus Andronicus*	Titus

1956

	Film	*The Prince and the Showgirl* (adaptation of *The Sleeping Prince*)	The Regent, Director (and producer)
Nov	Savoy	*Double Image*	Producer

1957

Apr	Royal Court	*The Entertainer*	Archie Rice
	Tour to Paris, Venice, Belgrade, Zagreb, Vienna and Warsaw with *Titus Andronicus*		
July	Stoll	*Titus Andronicus*	Titus
Sept	Palace	*The Entertainer*	Archie Rice
Apr	New	*Summer of the 17th Doll*	Producer

1958

Feb	Royale, New York	*The Entertainer*	Archie Rice
	Film	*The Devil's Disciple*	General Burgoyne
	ATV	*John Gabriel Borkman*	Borkman

1959

	Film	*The Entertainer*	Archie Rice
July	Memorial, Stratford	*Coliolanus*	Coriolanus
Sept	Duke of York's	*The Shifting Heart*	Producer

	NBC TV	*The Moon and Sixpence*	Charles Strickland
1960			
	Film	*Spartacus*	Crassus
	Helen Hayes, New York	*The Tumbler*	Director
Apr	Royal Court	*Rhinoceros*	Berenger
July	Strand	*Rhinoceros*	Berenger
Apr	Westminster	*A Lodging for a Bride*	Co-producer
Apr	Westminster	*Over the Bridge*	Co-producer
Oct	St James's, New York	*Becket*	Becket
1961			
	Film	*The Power and the Glory*	The Priest
Mar	On U.S. tour	*Becket*	Henry II
May	Hudson, New York	*Becket*	Henry II
1962			
	Film	*Term of Trial*	Graham Weir
July	Chichester Festival	*The Chances*	Director
July	Chichester Festival	*The Broken Heart*	Chorus, Bassanes, and Director
July	Chichester Festival	*Uncle Vanya*	Astrov, and Director
Dec	Saville	*Semi-Detached*	Fred Midway
1963			
July	Chichester Festival	*Uncle Vanya*	Astrov, and Director
	Film	*Uncle Vanya*	Astrov, and Director
Oct	Old Vic (National Theatre)	*Hamlet*	Director
Nov	Old Vic (NT)	*Uncle Vanya*	Astrov, and Director
Dec	Old Vic (NT)	*The Recruiting Officer*	Captain Brazen
1964			
Apr	Old Vic (NT)	*Othello*	Othello
July	Chichester Festival (NT)	*Othello*	Othello
Nov	Old Vic (NT)	*The Master Builder*	Solness (from Michael Redgrave)

1965
	Film	*Bunny Lake is Missing*	Inspector Newhouse
	Film	*Othello*	Othello
Jan	Old Vic (NT)	*The Crucible*	Director
Sept	Tour to Moscow and Berlin with *Othello* and *Love for Love*		
Oct	Old Vic (NT)	*Love for Love*	Tattle

1966
| | Film | *Khartoum* | The Mahdi |
| Apr | Old Vic (NT) | *Juno and the Paycock* | Director |

1967
| Feb | Old Vic (NT) | *The Dance of Death* | Captain Edgar |
| Apr | Old Vic (NT) | *The Three Sisters* | Director |

Tour of Canada with *The Dance of Death, Love for Love* and *A Flea in her Ear*, by Georges Feydeau, as Plucheux

1968
	Film	*The Shoes of the Fisherman*	Premier Kamenev
	Film	*The Dance of Death*	Captain Edgar
Sep	Old Vic (NT)	*The Advertisement*	Co–director
Dec	Old Vic (NT)	*Love's Labour's Lost*	Director

1969
	Film	*Oh! What a Lovely War*	Sir John French
	Film	*The Battle of Britain*	Sir Hugh Dowding
	Film	*David Copperfield*	Creakle
	Old Vic (NT)	*Home and Beauty*	A. B. Raham (from Arthur Lowe)
July	Old Vic (NT)	*The Three Sisters*	Director, and (later) Chebutikin (from Paul Curran)
July	Film	*The Three Sisters*	Director, and Chebutikin
	NBC TV	*Male of the Species*	Host/Narrator

1970
| Apr | Old Vic | *The Merchant of Venice* | Shylock |

1971

	Film	*Nicholas and Alexandra*	Count Witte
June	New (NT)	*Amphitryon 38*	Director
Dec	New (NT)	*Long Day's Journey Into Night*	James Tyrone
	ATV	*Long Day's Journey Into Night*	James Tyrone

1972

	Film	*Lady Caroline Lamb*	The Duke of Wellington
	Film	*Sleuth*	Andrew Wyke

1973

	ATV	*The Merchant of Venice*	Shylock
Oct	Old Vic (NT)	*Saturday, Sunday, Monday*	Antonio
Dec	Old Vic (NT)	*The Party*	John Tagg

1974

Apr	Old Vic (NT)	*Eden End*	Director

1975

	Film	*Love Among the Ruins*	Sir Arthur Granville-Jones

1976

	Film	*The Seven-Per-Cent Solution*	Moriarty
	Film	*Marathon Man*	Dr Christian Szell
	Granada TV	*The Collection*	Harry Kane (and co-producer)
	Granada TV	*Cat on a Hot Tin Roof*	Big Daddy (and co-producer)
	Granada TV	*Hindle Wakes*	Co-director

1977

	Film	*Jesus of Nazareth*	Nicodemus
	Film	*A Bridge Too Far*	Dr Spaander
	Granada TV	*Daphne Laureola*	Sir Joseph (and co-producer)
	Granada TV	*Come Back, Little Sheba*	Doc Delaney (and co-producer)

Granada TV	*Saturday, Sunday, Monday*	Antonio (and co-producer)

1978

Film	*The Betsy*	Loren Hardemann Sr
Film	*The Boys from Brazil*	Ezra Lieberman

1979

Film	*A Little Romance*	Julius
Film	*Dracula*	Professor Van Helsing

1980

St James's, New York	*Filumena*	Director

1980

Film	*The Jazz Singer*	Cantor Rabinovitch

1981

Film	*Clash of the Titans*	Zeus
Granada TV	*Brideshead Revisited*	Lord Marchmain

1982

Thames	*A Voyage Round My Father*	Clifford Mortimer

1983

Granada TV	*King Lear*	Lear
BBC TV	*A Talent for Murder*	Dr Wainwright

1984

Film	*The Bounty*	Admiral Hood
Film	*The Last Days of Pompeii*	Gaius
HTV	*Mr Halpern and Mr Johnson*	Mr Halpern
Granada TV	*The Ebony Tower*	Henry Breasley

1985

Film	*Wagner*	Sandor Lukacs
Film	*The Jigsaw Man*	Sir Gerald Scaith
Film	*Wild Geese II*	Rudolph Hess
Film	*Peter the Great*	King William III

1986

| Granada TV | *Lost Empires* | Harry Burrard |
| Dominion | *Time* | Portrayal of Akash |

INDEX

INDEX

The following abbreviations have been used: LO for Laurence Olivier; VL for Vivien Leigh